CONTENTS

Abbreviations	2
Introduction	3
Chapter 1: Backgrounds	4
Chapter 2: Garrison of East Pakistan	10
Chapter 3: The Pre-War War	17
Chapter 4: The Role of Foreign Powers	28
Chapter 5: Air and Naval Warfare	30
Chapter 6: Western Front, Indian Army's II Corps	38
Chapter 7: North-western Front, Indian Army's XXXIII Corps	44
Chapter 8: Northern Front, Indian Army's 101st Communications Zone	48
Chapter 9: Eastern Front, Indian Army's IV Corps	52
Chapter 10: Race to Dacca	59
Chapter 11: Conclusions	63
Bibliography	70
Endnotes	71

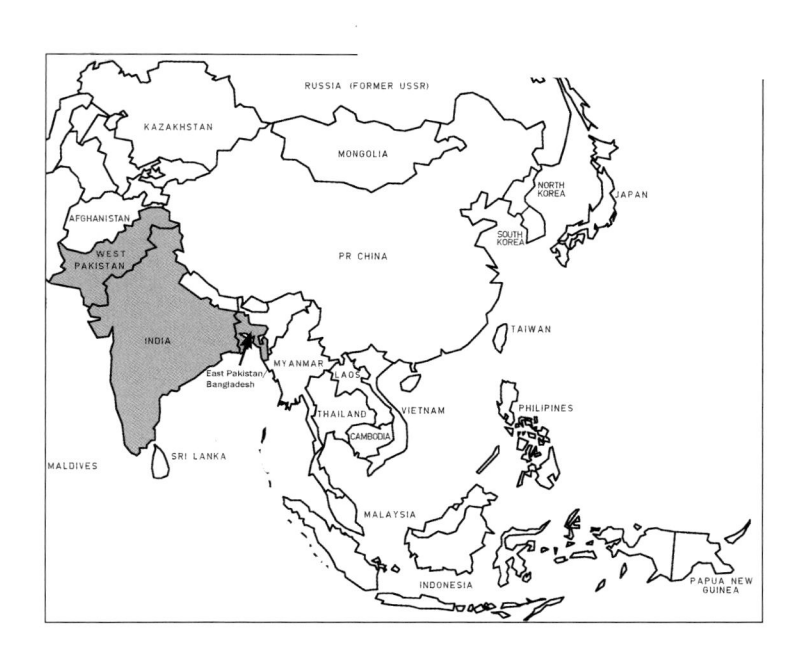

Helion & Company Limited
Unit 8 Amherst Business Centre
Budbrooke Road
Warwick
CV34 5WE
England
Tel. 01926 499 619
Email: info@helion.co.uk
Website: www.helion.co.uk
Twitter: @helionbooks
blog.helion.co.uk/

Published by Helion & Company 2020
Designed and typeset by Mach 3 Solutions Ltd (www.mach3solutions.co.uk)
Cover designed by Paul Hewitt, Battlefield Design (www.battlefield-design.co.uk)

Text © Ravi Rikhye 2020
Images © as individually credited
Colour profiles © Adrien Subtil, Luca Canossa, David Bocquelet, Tom Cooper 2020
Maps © Tom Cooper 2020

ISBN 978-1-913118-63-1

British Library Cataloguing-in-Publication Data.
A catalogue record for this book is available from the British Library.

All rights reserved. No part of this publication may be reproduced, stored in a retrieval system, or transmitted, in any form, or by any means, electronic, mechanical, photocopying, recording or otherwise, without the express written consent of Helion & Company Limited.

For details of other military history titles published by Helion & Company Limited contact the above address, or visit our website: http://www.helion.co.uk.

We always welcome receiving book proposals from prospective authors.

Front Cover Photograph

A PT-76 amphibious tank of the 45th Cavalry, Indian Army, rolling towards a Pakistan Army position in the Jessore area, after breaching enemy defences in the Chaugacha-Boyra area in late November or early December 1971. (Albert Grandolini Collection)

Front Cover Artwork

Heavy use in tropical climate quickly resulted in the quite 'dirty' overall appearance of Indian Air Force MiG-21s in 1971. This reconstruction of the example with the serial number C1111 from No. 4 Squadron shows the aircraft as it appeared shortly after the end of the 1971 war. Markings applied on the forward fuselage indicate that it flew a total of 26 combat sorties between 4 and 15 December 1971, and was involved in the destruction of three major targets (an ammunition factory outside Dacca, a bunker and a radio station). A silhouette atop the nose-markings commemorates an R-3S missile fired by Flight-Lieutenant J.S. Raj during air combat against an F-86E Sabre over Tezgaon (or Tejgaon) Air Base, north of Dacca, on 4 December 1971. (Artwork by Tom Cooper)

Note

In order to simplify the use of this book, all names, locations and geographic designations are as provided in *The Times World Atlas*, or other traditionally accepted major sources of reference, as of the time of the described events. For example, while the independence of Bangladesh was declared on 26 March 1971 – and this date is ever since celebrated as Independence Day – the country established itself as an independent nation only after the surrender of the Pakistani armed forces on 16 December 1971, the withdrawal of Indian armed forces on 12 March 1972 and the Simla/Shimla Agreement between India and Pakistan of 2 July 1972. Correspondingly, and to avoid confusion, for most of this narrative the country is named as per its official designation for the 1947–72 period, East Pakistan. Similarly, the official spelling of the capital city of Bangladesh was Dacca until 1983, when it was changed to Dhaka. When mentioned for the first time in the text, aircraft and heavy weapons system designations are cited fully – including their designer and/or the manufacturer, official military designation and nickname. In the case of Soviet-made armament, this is followed by the ASCC/NATO-codename, which is then used through the text.

Note on photographs: the majority of photographs used in this book were taken by Indian or foreign journalists, or official photographers, before, during and after the Indo-Pakistani War of 1971. Official organizations and news agencies in turn shared them with the Vietnam News Agency and the Military Museum of Hanoi, from where they found their way into the collection of Albert Grandolini.

Abbreviations

AB	air base
AK	Azad Kashmir Regiment
An	Antonov (the design bureau led by Oleg Antonov)
ASCC	Air Standardization Coordinating Committee
CO	commanding officer
COIN	counterinsurgency
COMINT	communications intelligence
EBR	East Bengal Regiment (regular units of the PA, staffed predominantly by Bengalis, later part of Bangladesh Army)
EPR	East Pakistan Rifles (paramilitary group)
FAC	fast attack craft (also 'missile boat')
FFR	Frontier Force Regiment (Pakistan Army)
GHQ	General Headquarters
GOI	Government of India
HQ	Headquarters
IAF	Indian Air Force
Il	Ilyushin (the design bureau led by Sergey Vladimirovich Ilyushin, also known as OKB-39)
ISI	Interservice Intelligence (top Pakistan intelligence agency)
KIA	killed in action
LST	landing ship tank (amphibious assault vessel carrying tanks)
MB	Mukti Bahini
MiG	Mikoyan i Gurevich (the design bureau led by Artyom Ivanovich Mikoyan and Mikhail Iosifovich Gurevich, also known as OKB-155 or MMZ 'Zenit')
PA	Pakistan Army
PAF	Pakistan Air Force
PRC	People's Republic of China (mainland China)
PLA	People's Liberation Army (of mainland China)
PLAAF	People's Liberation Army Air Force (of mainland China)
ORBAT	order of battle
R-3S	Soviet short-range AAM, ASCC codename AA-2 Atoll
RAF	Royal Air Force (of the United Kingdom)
RAW	Research and Analysis Wing (top Indian intelligence agency)
SAM	surface-to-air missile
SFF	Special Frontier Force (special forces asset of the Indian Army)
SIGINT	signals intelligence
SSG	Special Service Group (special forces asset of the Pakistan Army)
Su	Sukhoi (the design bureau led by Pavel Ossipovich Sukhoi, also known as OKB-51)
USA	United States of America

INTRODUCTION

The India–Pakistan War of 1971 was a short, but bitter and relatively complex war, fought in two entirely separate campaigns. As of 1947–71, Pakistan was – geographically and economically – a unique country, divided into two wings separated by 1,600km as the crow flies, and 5,500 nautical kilometres along the shortest sea route. The country was plagued by imbalance between the two parts right from its creation: the territory of West Pakistan was almost six times larger than East Pakistan. West Pakistan contained the nation's capital, where all the political power was concentrated, including an almost total monopoly of appointments in the civil service, armed forces and the diplomatic service, although its population was outnumbered by three to one by the East.

On the contrary, established in the rich alluvial plains formed by the confluence of three major rivers – the Brahmaputra, Ganges and Meghna – and their tributaries, East Pakistan accounted for 75 percent of exports and foreign earnings. However, it received less than 30 percent of the nation's imports and investment, and had a per capita income lower than in the West. For all practical reasons and purposes, the rulers of Pakistan treated the East as a colony that was milked continuously. Finding such behaviour increasingly intolerable, the Easterners attempted to negotiate: the military junta in Islamabad reacted with empty promises and brutal suppression, driving the Easterners to move their demands away from the idea of autonomy towards total separation. By 1970, the situation drove Islamabad to apply the policy of overkill with a vengeance, aimed at intimidating the population of the East into submission. The outrageous behaviour of the Pakistan Army (PA) had unforeseen results: with nothing to lose, the local population fought back, while many thousands fled across the border into India. Miscalculating that the People's Republic of China (PRC) and the United States of America (USA) would enable it to counter any threat that India might pose, Islamabad increased the pressure. However, convinced that events in East Pakistan posed the biggest threat for its security since 1947, and facing indifference in the United Nations, New Delhi concluded the situation was intolerable: while starting to provide support for the insurgency in East Pakistan, it mobilised its armed forces for war. Although in possession of overwhelming military superiority, the Pakistan Army was facing a hostile population that resisted at every opportunity, and the weather proved of vital influence: no intervention could occur before the end of the monsoon season in November 1971, when the ground in East Pakistan would be dry enough to enable large-scale operations, and the onset of the winter would close the Sino-Indian frontier. Unsurprisingly, as soon as the Indian Navy blockaded East Pakistan, its fate was a foregone conclusion.

Because there was no way Pakistan could defeat or even stall the Indians, to tell the story of the East Pakistan campaign alone is not particularly instructive. It is necessary to also understand the strategic, political and international backgrounds before and during the war. There are also lessons to be learned; the most important of which is that political objectives must match military capability. As India learned to its great cost during the 1962 Sino–Indian War, going unprepared into a war and telling the soldiers they must hold to the last man is not a useful strategy. Operating in a crisis when all odds are adverse requires exceptionally ruthless and clear-headed leaders, both political and military. As was the case for India in 1962, in 1971 Pakistan refused to adjust its political aims to its military capabilities: after choosing ruthlessness early on, its leaders chose the softest options; and instead of clear-headedness, they retreated into fantasies. They sacrificed the lives of thousands of soldiers and succeeded only in inflicting a permanent trauma on their national psyche. This is a criminal act, one for which no one was punished. Ironically, India went through an opposite process: while facing China in 1962, India had three years to prepare but its political leaders mistook their fantastic illusions for reality. In 1971, Pakistan had just eight months; it needed more, and it had the means to hold the crisis at bay for many more months. But because of their arrogance, which gave birth to ideas such as that the 'physically weak Bengalis could be easily cowed', they went into a war with minimal preparation.

For India, the 1971 war was a huge psychological victory, almost a chiliastic event: it was said poetically that for the first time in a thousand years, the Hindus had defeated the Muslims. That is not historically true, as Hindu armies defeated the Muslims many times. Nonetheless, that is the way Indians felt, and still feel. Equally important, the Indian Army performed at a high level of skill and efficiency never seen before in the nation's three previous wars since Independence – 1947–48 in Kashmir, 1962 against China and 1965 against Pakistan.

A major problem in researching and writing about the Indo–Pakistan War of 1971 is that there is not much primary and authoritative information available, while second-hand reference materials are often too costly for an amateur historian to acquire: out-of-print Pakistani books, for example, usually sell for US$100 and more. Even if acquirable, different books disagree with each other in regards of details – and none is based on official documentation. Indeed, both the Indians and the Pakistanis have destroyed their related records; the Pakistanis before surrendering, and the Indians a few years after the war. Moreover, the mass of second-hand reference materials are one-sided. As a result, only enough material is available to generalise, and much of the work presented here is, undoubtedly, simplified – due to attempts to make a coherent story.

Another issue is that many books and articles were written well after the war, and memories are fading. This is of particular importance considering that neither India nor Pakistan at that time had an open culture about military matters, and criticism of military affairs remains a *de-facto* taboo in both countries until this very day. The official Indian history of the 1971 war was never authorised, despite treading softly on things that were obviously done wrong, or could have been done better within the limits of the day. In turn, because they lost, the Pakistanis are slightly more rigorous in their criticism, even if carefully avoiding assigning blame for failures. Eventually, the list of recommended reference literature can be limited to about a dozen core works. Sisson and Rose have provided a detailed overview, and Srinath Raghvan an overview from the Indian side. The latter author provided another book, which analyses the history of US–Indian relations. The two best books on the military campaign were published by Sukhwant Singh on the Indian side and Salik on the Pakistani side. Other invaluable works were published by Farman Ali, F.M. Khan and G.W. Choudhary. Finally, there are a few books worth attention for those who want to dig deeper. For the Indian Air Force (IAF), Jagan Mohan and Samir Chopra have provided the best coverage. Their work provides material from the Pakistani side, too, and easily meets any standards for a campaign history. For a concise study with good maps and Indian order of battle (ORBAT), John Gill's work stands out. Last, but not least, there are the 'unpublished' official Indian history of the war and my own unpublished doctoral thesis on US–Indo relations during the 1971 crisis: sadly, I never found the money necessary to pay the related tuition fees.[1]

CHAPTER 1
BACKGROUNDS

Arabs have traded with India since 3000 BC. When Islam emerged in Arabia, the traders included missionaries, who began voluntary conversion of Hindus who felt oppressed in their caste system. Historians do not like to discuss what happened next in terms of Hindus and Muslims, because the latter were of different ethnicities – Arab, Turk, Afghani and Central Asian being the main ones. For an overview, however, the religious labels have greater explanatory power. Inevitably, militant Islamic invaders came to loot the fabulously rich land of India, but were held west of the Indus River by confederations of Indian kings until about 1000 AD. In the 12th century, Muslim kings broke through. Indian monarchs had returned to their incessant, internecine warfare that characterised the subcontinent since the dawn of recorded history. A major difference was that Muhammad Ghori was looking for a kingdom not just to loot. With the Hindu kings more focused on fighting each other, within barely four decades, the Muslims became established in India by the end of the 12th century. Their expansion continued – with the help of Hindu kings who still were more interested in enlisting the foreigner to settle accounts with their Hindu adversaries. Within 400 years, Muslim kings dominated India until the British began to arrive in 1600. The Indians – regardless of religion – immediately involved the white invader and his well-trained armies in local disputes, gaining short-term victory without understanding that British help came at a price. In a repeat of the old fable of the camel getting his nose under the tent, the British East India Company began building its own empire. It was certainly the case that 'the flag follows trade', and for 250 years it was Great Britain that controlled India.

In 1857, tired of increasingly oppressive British rule designed to extract the maximum amount of money from India, Muslims and Hindus alike mutinied against British rule. Ironically, though 80 percent of the rebel soldiers were Hindus, the British blamed the Muslims for the revolt. This was because – as related by Agha H. Amin – the rebellion was led by the predominantly Muslim cavalry, especially Meerut regiments, who constituted just 5 percent of the regiments the East India Company's armies. Eighty percent of cavalry went to Delhi and Lucknow, and the hardest fighting was at Delhi, where 90 percent of British casualties were incurred. Moreover, the Muslim rebels proclaimed the revival of the defunct Mughal Empire, whose emperor resided in Delhi. In British eyes, the Muslims became the public face of the rebellion and were henceforth marginalised in favour of Hindus: ironically, most Indians – regardless of religion – remained uninvolved and at least passively loyal to the British.

Subsequently, the British spread their style of education throughout India, both for practical and idealistic reasons: practical because the Empire needed local enablers, and idealistic because many British genuinely believed in 'uplifting the masses'. The Hindus, however, learned from their British masters too well: by the end of the 19th century, the Hindu Indian elite were invested in the idea of democracy and independence. Always loyal to the motto 'divide and rule', as a counterbalance, the British shifted their favour to the Muslims. Nonetheless, although some Muslims wanted their own nation in India, others considered the Hindus and Muslims as people of the same nation.

Partition of India

Undaunted, early during the 20th century, the British began suggesting separate legislative seats for the two religions, which further solidified Muslim thoughts of an independent nation. Above all, the fear that the Hindus would rule over them was abhorrent to the Muslims.[1] The movement for independence kept growing. Moreover, the Muslims believed they were the natural rulers of India, even though on the millennium scales of Indian history they were relative newcomers. The Muslims had no problems accepting the whites as their overlords, but – due to racism – could not accept living in a Hindu-dominated India. Admittedly, the 'Muslims' in question were not all the Muslim people living on the sub-continent but only a tiny 'elite' that also interpreted Islam as mandating a theocracy. The Hindu elite which led the move for independence, with few exceptions, believed the natural state of South Asia was for Muslims and Hindus to live together peacefully as citizens of a democratic India. What followed is a long and sad tale of action and reaction: even as late as 1946, a year before partition, the demand for an independent Pakistan did not dominate the Muslim psyche. However, it happened because the Muslim elite could not bring themselves to trust the Hindu majority: explaining this is difficult because the ideas of different politicians changed almost day-to-day to accommodate a myriad of interests.

Though Indians blame Britain for partition, stressing it was part of their policy of 'divide and rule', the evidence shows that the British wanted a strong, united Indian dominion as an ally, particularly to hold back the Soviets. They followed divide and rule to maintain their paramountcy of India. Since they were leaving, however, a united Indian dominion loyal to the British Crown was seen as 'ideal'.

Independence

Aside from the growing demand from Indians for freedom, the British were bankrupt and unable to afford the six extra brigades of troops to hold India. Since their defeat by the Japanese in 1942, the myth of white superiority was shattered, and events such as the Royal Indian Navy Mutiny of 1946 alarmed them greatly. In retrospect, a 10-year interregnum was preferable where internal differences would be resolved and a peaceful solution found to the problem of the Muslim minority. With Nazi Germany and Japan defeated, the British conscript army wanted to go home. The British ruled India with a handful of civil servants and troops because of a carefully crafted shadow play of their omnipotence and irresistible power, again using divide and rule. With that myth in ruins, the Indians realised it was only their cooperation with the British that had permitted the colonial masters to run a subcontinent with a population of 450 million. The British became genuinely concerned for their safety and wanted to leave. Moreover, the USA had exerted immense pressure on London to permit Indian independence. Some of the reasons were altruistic: the Second World War had been fought by the Allies as a crusade for freedom, and in 1945, the United Nations enshrined the right of self-determination for colonised people. Other reasons were practical by nature: the Americans were convinced that India's willing cooperation had been imperative in the defeat of Imperial Japan.

At the time, and with the British military rapidly demobilising and its treasury empty, London was also faced with the problem of maintaining control over the Middle East and its vital oil supplies. Palestine alone required two divisions to hold. Because the Union of Soviet Socialist Republics (USSR) not only overran Eastern Europe, but began threatening Berlin and West Germany, and then expressing interest in becoming involved abroad, the British felt forced to return a division to Europe and bolster its small forces there. Finally, the British Empire still had to man a number of far-flung garrisons around the world. It may seem odd that the British – who in the Second World War had the third biggest army, the second largest navy and possibly the third largest air force – could not find two divisions to keep India pacified. But six years of war had exhausted the British, and they saw no advantage in helping an India that wanted them to leave and a peaceful transition to independence.

Muslims did not start out wanting an independent homeland. Rather, they sought a confederation with central government's powers limited to external affairs, defence and communications, with remaining powers devolved to the states. The Congress Party, heading the independence movement, wanted a tightly centralised country, because it did not desire a return to a traditional India of multiple competing states. Such a tightly centralised nation was unacceptable to Muslims. Consequently, these competing visions created the final break.

Carving out Pakistan

In 1940, the Muslim League, the main Muslim political party, called for a division of India into three independent parts: a Muslim West Pakistan, a Muslim East Pakistan, and the rest of India for the Hindus and minorities. It is no coincidence that the name 'Pakistan' stood for

P = Punjab
A = Afghania (North-West Frontier Province)
K = Kashmir
I = Iran (more specifically Baluchistan, which is divided between Pakistan and Iran)
S = Sindh

'Stan' means 'place', and 'Pakistan' means 'the Land of the Pure'. Ironically, and right from the start, there was no mention of Bengal – the area with the biggest Muslim population on the Indian Subcontinent – nor that of Baluchistan. Up to 1946, Muhammad Ali Jinnah, the leading Indian Muslim politician, saw no reason to deny an independent East Pakistan, but in his view West Bengal and Assam had to be included in this 'second Pakistan'. The Hindus refused to accept this because they believed they would be oppressed – as indeed they were from 1940 to 1971. In 1946, the demand for two independent Muslim states was changed to a unitary Pakistan – split into western and eastern wings, intended to be the sole representative of all the Muslims on the subcontinent.[2] Furthermore, Jinnah came to feel that an independent East Pakistan would vitiate his idea of a single homeland for 'all' Muslims. In reality, the idea of a country separated by 1,600km – and 5,000km by sea – made as much sense as a united Ireland and Poland, just because both are predominantly Catholic; even more so as the people's wishes had nothing to do with this decision. Nevertheless, the British helpfully pointed out to Jinnah, who created Pakistan, that without the tax revenues of the East, West Pakistan would not be a viable state. Curiously, although one might expect that after controlling India for 250 years the British might know better, nobody in London came to the conclusion that such a construction was illogical in the first place – even more so because to the Bengalis it was their language that was the core of their identity, an issue that took precedence over almost everything. Nevertheless, Urdu was declared the official language of the new nation – at the time, only 8 percent of its population spoke Urdu as a first language: indeed, after Bengali, Punjabi was the second tongue.

It therefore must be concluded that the partition of India was an illogical, badly thought-out exercise, conducted in a great hurry. Unsurprisingly, the Bengalis of East Pakistan did not accept the unitary state right from the start. They went along with the concept because it was sprung on them at the last minute, just months before independence, because everyone was confused and made compromises which later proved untenable. The East Bengalis wanted independence, or at the least a minimal confederation of West and East, and they never gave up that dream.

Blunders Welcome

Matters might still have worked, had the Bengalis been given political power proportionate to their numbers. The West

Punjabis, and particularly the Army, were having none of this. The West treated the East as a colony – which was nothing but ironic, considering decolonisation and giving freedom to the people were the principal ideas of the United Nations. On the contrary, the Bengalis were not even allowed their own language, with Urdu being declared the official language of the entire Pakistan. Though East Pakistan's Bengalis were in a majority, they were forced to accept the same number of seats in Parliament as West Pakistan. The Army was also Punjabi-dominated: barely two battalions were recruited from Bengal. The number of military officers and civil servants from Bengal was less than 10 percent, whereas Bengalis made up 55 precent of the population. That the Punjabis also discriminated against others in West Pakistan's provinces in the matter of language was, of course, no solace to the Bengalis. The West took the bulk of the East's foreign exchange earnings and international aid too, further impoverishing an already poor province.

The reason for West Pakistan's discrimination against the East lay in simple racism. Indian Muslims thought of themselves as tall, fair and warlike. They believed they were 'true Muslims', while the Bengalis – dark, short and physically unimposing – were 'too infected with Hinduism to be true Muslims'. The powerful Muslim lords in Bengal claimed Afghan, Turk, and Central Asian ancestry. Correspondingly, President Ayub Khan, who ruled Pakistan as its second president from 1958–69, spent much of his time making sure the Bengalis were kept politically suppressed. An example is his attempts to have the Bengalis write in Arabic script, or to have Pakistan's currency notes printed in West Pakistan languages but not in Bengali. Aside from the unequal distribution of economic resources in the western wing's favour, Bengalis were deliberately deprived of the opportunity to join the military and central civil service, both of which were dominated by the Punjabis.

Matters started to come to a head after the 1965 war, when the Bengalis realised Islamabad had no plans to defend the East. This issue demands a closer look. Had India not held its hand in 1965, it could have occupied large parts of East Pakistan with relative ease. As it happened, the administration of President Lyndon B. Johnson in Washington asked New Delhi not to expand the war to the East, and India obliged. India thought it more important to keep the USA happy in case China intervened in the 1965 war, than to seize parts of East Pakistan it would have to return at the war's end. One need not be a Marxist to conclude that West Pakistan's 24-year economic exploitation of East Pakistan underlay everything else, causing an immense antagonism toward the West.

Appearance and Reality of the East Pakistan Revolt

The conventional narrative of how East Pakistan came to revolt against West Pakistan is that when President Yahya Khan decided to restore democracy in 1970, East Bengal won a majority of seats in the national assembly. Accordingly, both Yahya Khan and Zulfikar Ali Bhutto (who headed the second largest party in West Pakistan, and all of whose members were from the West) refused to accept the Bengali leader, Mujib Rehman, as a Prime Minister of Pakistan. Indeed, Bhutto and Yahya then conspired to invalidate the election, at which point the Bengalis revolted. This narrative is accepted even today, 50 years later, because it is a simple and easily understood story.

Tragically, this narrative happens to be untrue. Right from 1948, people like Mujibar Rehman – then a student leader – were working toward separation for East Pakistan. Well before the 1970 election, Mujib's Awami League was pushing for partition. In 1966, he and several others were put under arrest for conspiracy to secede using violence. Mujib was released before the election because Yahya knew how popular he was, and Yahya did not want to stage a rigged election. Indeed, the election was certified as fair by foreign observers – something for which Yahya received no credit. Later, it was said that Yahya did not anticipate that Mujibar would win, implying Yahya held a bad-faith election. This also is not true. Yahya had received multiple warnings – foremost from the omni-present Interservice Intelligence (ISI) of Pakistan – that Mujib would win, but still insisted on going ahead with the election. And when Mujib won, Yahya met Mujib to work out any compromise that would give the Bengalis what they wanted if they remained in a united Pakistan, even if only in name. Some observers, such as the Pakistan President's advisor on East Pakistan, G.W. Choudhry (himself a Bengali), believed Mujib would have accepted a united Pakistan, with himself as the prime minister, a position to which he was entitled because his Awami League party won the majority of seats in the 1970 election.[3]

Nevertheless, the Bengali people wanted independence. Indeed, Mujib had run on that platform, openly speaking for independence, even as in his talks with Yahya he spoke of a 'united nation'. While appearing two-faced, he was not: he had spent four years in jail after being arrested for secessionism, and was too aware the Pakistani Army could put him right back in prison again – and probably execute him too. Thus, he spoke of compromise to protect his life. His 'six points', on which he had run for the past 24 years, called for a federation of East and West Pakistan, a separate East Pakistan currency and reserve bank, a separate military, communications and trade. It was this platform that won the hearts and aspirations of tens of millions of Bengalis. Had he compromised on the 'six points', his followers would have dumped him.

As an example of the simmering anger, when Lieutenant Colonel H. Qureshi came to take over the 26th Battalion of the Frontier Force Regiment (FFR) in late August 1970 (shortly before the December election), he found there were orders that officers could not move about East Pakistan without an armed military escort: West Pakistani soldiers and officers were already being attacked in the street and thus confined to their bases. Local vendors also refused to sell them vegetables, fruit and milk.[4] Notable Pakistan defence historian Hamid Hussain says that while soldiers were not being killed, they were constantly harassed and abused (as we will see, this was the primary reason why when they got a chance to hit back, they committed many atrocities). Mujib was already saying he would not compromise on his 'six points', and his Awami League party was already in the process of taking over the civil administration after the election – and ruthlessly eliminating parties that opposed his platform. Since the civil administration was largely Bengali, not only was it acting at the Awami League's behest, but it was providing secret documents to the League. Because Yahya had ordered the Army to stand strictly aside during the elections, it could do nothing when other parties came to it to say vote fixing was going on. And when on 1 March 1971 the National Assembly was postponed because of a failure between West and East Pakistan to reach agreement on remaining united, anarchy descended, the Awami League taking open control of the government in the East and Mujib announcing that East Pakistan had declared independence.

Even then, an 'open break' took place only on 25 March 1971, when President Yahya Khan ordered a crackdown to bring East Pakistan to heel. Even this, however, only happened because the Bengalis had revolted already on 1 March, and Mujib Rehman's word was followed, not that of the Pakistan Army. Mutinies began in earnest, including the killing of West Pakistani soldiers and their families. From the West Pakistani point of view, it was imperative to quickly re-establish control. Thus, while historians have spent shiploads of ink to show that it was the crackdown that led to a final break, it is fair to say that the movement for independence built up throughout 1970, when Yahya permitted the resumption of political activity. The 1 March postponement of the National Assembly was the point of the final break, not 26 March. So set on independence were Mujib and his supporters that no matter what was decided after the December 1970 elections, Mujib would not have been able to force any agreement for unified Pakistan on his followers – even if he was inclined, which he was not. As Qureshi wrote, the West Pakistanis were passively living in an imaginary world. They could not see the reality of the situation, that Pakistan was breaking up, so the Pakistan Army's General Headquarters (GHQ) simply shut its eyes.[5]

Was it moral for East Pakistan to revolt?

According to internationally accepted laws, foremost the UN Charter, East Pakistan had no right to secede without its population deciding to do so in a referendum. Equally, a point most Indians remain unaware of is that valid international laws gave India no right to break up Pakistan. Indeed, 1971 was the first time this happened since the UN was established in 1945. But there is the legal case and there is the moral right. A case can be made that East Pakistan had a moral right to secede. The primary reason people band together in nations is to gain protection from violence, both external and internal. For this service, people pay taxes – 10 percent of GDP is fair. A second reason is that they expect the state, in exchange for the taxes people pay, to provide services such as roads, ports, schools and hospitals which individuals cannot provide. For that, another 10 percent of GDP paid in taxes is fair. In the 20th century, a third reason arose: the state must ensure the wellbeing of its people. The additional taxes for developed nations today bring the total tax burden to between 40 percent (USA) and 60 percent (France) of GDP in taxes. If West Pakistan could not provide national security for East Pakistan, the major reason for the legitimacy of the state was vitiated. And if the government could not provide basics like roads, schools and hospitals, the

One of many pro-independence protests in early March 1971. Similar demonstrations were organised by those who wanted to remain with Pakistan – even if on a much smaller scale. (Albert Grandolini Collection)

second reason was violated too. In 1971, and particularly for poor countries, the right of people to be looked after by the state was not particularly relevant because the money was lacking. Nevertheless, the people had the right to expect the state to help in case of extreme calamity. Here too, East Bengal believed the government had failed it after the massive Bhola typhoon hit the province in mid-November 1970. Interestingly, President Yahya was so committed to elections he refused to postpone them, and they were held on schedule. It is likely the great anger Bengalis subsequently felt toward the government played a significant part in the vote.

Furthermore, the people of West Pakistan decided – without consulting anybody in East Pakistan – that 13 divisions of the Army should be reserved for the West, and only one must suffice for the people of the East. When two additional divisions were sent to East Pakistan, it was to repress the revolt, not to protect the East from India. Though West Pakistan planned to redress the inequality of resources it had created by taking most of the foreign aid and investments for 25 years, the East had built up a deep grievance against the West.

East Pakistan also had another point in its favour, both legal and moral: it had wanted its own country upon partition. This had been denied to them; indeed, partition itself was illegal because except for a sliver of Indians, no one was given a chance to say where they wanted to go. Either the British should have insisted the country remain united, or they should have permitted a general referendum on separation, with equal votes for everyone. It can be argued legally and morally that since the people of East Bengal did not choose to be part of Pakistan upon independence, they did have a right of secession. However, the same was (and remains) valid for Kashmir, too, where the people were also never given the opportunity to express their decision. This all still leaves India in the legal wrong – even if there is no doubt that in the 50 years since partition, many member states of the UN have busily rearranged other people's countries to suit their own interests. Considering what the Western powers were doing all over the world, it is hard to condemn India, but the fact remains: before 1971, no country had forcibly split another.

Coercion by Misinformation

The longer the crisis in East Pakistan went on, the more the government in Islamabad found itself exposed to coercion by misinformation. Examples were numerous, but the best-known include the Pakistani opponents claiming that three million Bengalis had been murdered, and 200,000 women raped. Not to be outdone, New Delhi used such claims to justify its intervention, adding that its politically, strategically and economically fragile north-east could end up being overrun by up to 20 million refugees. In reality, the number of refugees streaming into India never reached even the more recently – and officially – issued figure of 10 million.[6] For comparison, sources within intelligence circles have stressed an estimation of 4 million, most of whom were *de-facto* economic migrants. One should keep in mind not only that East Pakistan was very poor, but that it was also subject to repeated, and immense, natural disasters. Thus, there was an incentive to migrate to India – other than the war.[7]

Nevertheless, through such behaviour, India was directly coercing Pakistan and the international community: it was

Sheikh Mujibar Rahman (left) with Zulfiqar Ali Bhutto during a meeting at the Hotel Intercontinental in Dacca, January 1971. (Albert Grandolini Collection)

justifying its military intervention although this was against international law, and it was attracting international support – for itself and for the insurgency it decided to support. Nationalist Bengalis did their share of rape, loot and murder of civilians – especially those backing West Pakistan – and, regardless of who did what, the Hindu population of East Pakistan decreased from 30 percent in 1970 to only 10 percent two years later.

Body of Proof

There is hardly a Pakistani analyst or academic who has failed to blame India for precipitating the breakup of Pakistan – and they are all right. Nonetheless, as India found after the 1971 war – when it tried to repeat the exercise by instilling a breakaway of Sindh and Baluchistan from Pakistan – an external power cannot break up a country if the majority of its people are united. This remains valid notwithstanding the fact that Pakistan has never learned from its own failure while supporting insurgencies in the Punjab, and then in Kashmir. Right from Independence on 14 August 1948, West and East Pakistan could never remain united, because the Easterners did not want to remain united: they failed to separate in 1954, and then Pakistan did not break up in 1966, but it did break up on the next inflexion date in 1970–71.

To remain fair, it must be stressed that India bore East Pakistan no animus: Pakistan, which has never accepted the accession of Kashmir to India, saw its chance to cooperate with China as retaliation for what Pakistan saw as the forced annexation of Kashmir to India since 1947. Moreover, Pakistan's major ally, China, was giving assistance to North-East Indian rebel tribes which had been largely left alone by the British. These tribes, principally the militant Nagas, had revolted as early as 1956, and the Indian Army embarked on a 30-year counterinsurgency which eventually resulted in the complete integration of the Nagas into India. Later, the Chinese also began assisting Mizo rebels. Chinese intervention began before the 1962 Sino–India War, and accelerated afterward. By the end of that decade, East Pakistan became the base for assistance to Indian rebels. India retaliated by teaming up Bangladesh nationalists. Although on all three sides – India, China and Pakistan – the interventions were at a very low level, they were still taking place. It is thus unsurprising that East Pakistani dissidents were in touch with Indian intelligence from the 1960s onward.

Table 1: Indo–Pakistan War 1971, Top Political and Military Figureheads

Position	Military Rank & Name	Notes
West Pakistan		
President of Pakistan	General Yahya Khan	
Commander-in-Chief Pakistan Armed Forces and General Officer Commanding, Eastern Command, Dacca	Lieutenant General Amir Abdullah Khan Niazi	Eastern Command planned to become the III Corps, PA
Chief-of-Staff, Pakistan Armed Forces	Major General M. Rahim Khan	
Governor of Pakistan	Vice Admiral Syed Mohammad Ashsan	
Advisor to Governor	Major General Rao Farman Ali Khan	
General Officer Commanding, 14th Division, PA	Major General Khadim Asan Raza	
Chief Martial Law Administrator, East Pakistan	Brigadier Gulam Jilani Khan	
Leader of the second-largest party, West Pakistan	Zulfiqar Ali Bhutto	
East Pakistan/Bangladesh		
Prime Minister	Tajuddin Ahmed	
Prime Minister elect	Sheikh Mujibar Rehman	Winner of December 1970 election, waiting to assume the office
Commander, Armed Forces of Bangladesh	Colonel M.A.G. Osmani	Former PA officer
India		
President, Prime Minister and Commander-in-Chief Armed Forces of India	Indira Gandhi	
Minister of Defence	Jagjivan Ram	
Head of Prime Minister Office and Senior Advisor	P.N. Haksar	
Director General, Border Security Force	K.L. Rustomji	
Director Research and Analysis Wing (RAW)	Rameshwar Nath Kao	
Commander of Army	General Hormusji Framji Jamshedji 'Sam' Manekshaw	
Commander of Navy	Admiral Sardarilal Mathradas Nanda	
Commander of Air Force	Air Chief Marshal Pratap Chandra Lal	
Commander, Eastern Command	Lieutenant General Jagjit Singh Aurora	Eastern Command was also known as 'Eastern Army'
Chief-of-Staff, Eastern Command	Major General Jack Farj Rafael Jacob	
General Officer Commanding, II Corps	Lieutenant General Tapishwar Narain Raina	
General Officer Commanding, IV Corps	Lieutenant General Sagat Singh	
General Officer Commanding, XXXIII Corps	Lieutenant General M.L. Thapan	
General Officer Commanding, 101st Communications Zone	Major General Gurbax Singh Gill	

CHAPTER 2
GARRISON OF EAST PAKISTAN

In complete ignorance of millennia-old military traditions of India and Pakistan; the fact that India provided the fourth-largest troop contingent to defeat the Axis powers during the Second World War; the fact that India has consistently supported UN peace-keeping operations in Korea, Vietnam, Laos, the Congo and the Middle East in the 1950s and 1960s; but because of the Indian policy of determined neutralism ever since the Cold War, Western observers are still frequently caught guessing why two such 'under-developed nations' as India and Pakistan maintain such massive armed forces as they do. As is so often the case, there are many answers to such a question, yet none of them are simple.

India's principal policies since independence were to maintain the boundaries as drawn in colonial days and by the 1947 partition, to hold Jammu and Kashmir against Pakistan's claims, to unify and rule its diverse population, and to eliminate any foreign enclaves along its coasts, or insurgencies. The defeat by China in 1962 caused a complete reappraisal of Indian defence policy and resulted in a massive build-up of its armed forces and defence industries: the former were doubled in size. While primarily aimed at deterring Chinese aggression, this build-up in turn stimulated Pakistan into attempting to gain Kashmir before India became too powerful, leading to the Indo–Pakistani War of 1965. Subsequently, it prompted Islamabad into replacing quality with quantity while nearly doubling the size of its armed forces – despite endemic political, economic and social problems plaguing the country since 1947. Initially sponsored by the British, Pakistan's security arrangements were heavily sponsored by the USA, which provided up to US$2.8 billion from 1954–70. Following the Western arms embargo imposed in 1965, Turkey, Iran and Indonesia aided Pakistan with shipments of arms, ammunition, vehicles and spare parts. Subsequently, China took over with generous provision of tanks, aircraft and artillery; while cautious not to damage its relations with New Delhi, even the USSR sent trucks and helicopters – most of this free of charge. Meanwhile, although consuming up to 40 percent of the federal annual budget, Indian defence spending rarely reached more than 3 percent of the Gross National Product, and usually resembled the minimum acceptable on a risk basis. Contrary to Pakistan, India began receiving grant aid from the USA only after its war with China, in 1962, when Washington agreed to provide equipment – including transport aircraft surplus to its requirements – worth US$200 million. Only US$85 million of this was provided before deliveries were stopped due to the arms embargo of 1965. While purchasing arms worth more than US$1.2 billion from the Soviet Union in the period 1965–70, India insisted on paying for these by any means available – including its own currency and commodities – instead of accepting the political influence of Moscow.[1] As a result of all of this, by 1971, both India and Pakistan were in control of a massive conventional force, but there was still no doubt about the overwhelming Indian superiority.

Strategic Imbalance

A breakdown by divisions and approximate raising years – as provided in Table 2 – helps set the background for the East Pakistan campaign of 1971, and shows why Pakistan's defeat was inevitable. Essentially,

a) The USA refused to pay for more than 5½ divisions of the PA (the 12th Division was not counted as part of the regular army at the time, because it operated under the fictitious explanation that it was composed of Azad (free) Kashmiris fighting for the liberty of their homeland): this was the number of units the Pentagon calculated would be necessary to hold off a Soviet invasion until US forces could be deployed to help.

b) Not seriously concerned by a Soviet invasion, the GHQ in Rawalpindi and thus the government in Islamabad concluded they were hopelessly outmatched *vis-à-vis* India, and in late 1970 planned to raise two divisions (the 17th and 33rd) equipped with Chinese armaments (which had already equipped three divisions – the 9th, 16th and 18th).[2] The establishment of two further divisions (the 35th and 37th) was initiated in November 1971, but came too late, while one (the 23rd) was raised in 1971 using existing units, and deployed to shorten the 400km area of responsibility of the 12th Division.[3]

Thus, as of December 1971, and regardless of the Chinese arms being provided for free, the Pakistan Army had 15 divisions versus India's 25 – a dangerous imbalance (even more so considering India's Gross Domestic Product was at least six times that of Pakistan).[4] Still, and while knowing the entire country was stressed for resources, the leaders in Rawalpindi were not overly concerned: they expected to count on Beijing to tie down the Indian Army in the north. They also trusted in the self-propagated myth that every one of their soldiers was worth three or more Indian troops.[5]

Even had China stepped in, to balance India's strength Islamabad would need at least 15 operational divisions in West Pakistan and three in East Pakistan, a total of at least 18 divisions, and preferably 20–25 – provided it could balance Indian firepower on its own. Even then, this was unlikely to happen, because the Indian Navy and Indian Air Force were at least three times bigger than those of Pakistan's (see Tables 2, 8 and 9). Furthermore, Islamabad should have known better than to expect that China would join it in a war with India: since the Cultural Revolution initiated in the mid-1960s, the entire PRC was in a state of chaos, rendering large parts of its armed forces ineffective.

Table 2: New Raisings of Indian Army and Pakistan Army Divisions

Period	Indian Army	Pakistan Army
1947	4th and 5th Divisions	None
1948	1st Armoured, 19th and 26th Divisions	6th, 7th, 8th, 9th, 10th, 12th, 14th and 15th Divisions
By 1953	20th, 23rd, 25th and 27th Divisions	None
By 1959	17th Division	1st Armoured, but 6th and 9th Divisions disbanded
1962	2nd, 3rd and 8th Divisions	None
By 1965	6th, 7th, 9th, 10th, 11th, 12th, 14th, 15th, 23rd, 36th, 39th, 54th and 57th Divisions	6th Armoured and 11th Division
1966	None	9th, 16th and 18th Divisions
By 1971	None	17th, 23rd, 33rd, 35th and 37th Divisions – all working up

Military and Security Forces of East Pakistan

Major General Farman Ali, who had been in East Pakistan since 1967, was thoroughly familiar with the local situation and quietly sympathetic to the Bengalis. He was among several senior officers who urged a compromise but was ignored because the hardliners tied Yahya's hands. Farman Ali's official position in 1971 was civil-political advisor to the governor, himself a Bengali with no heart for oppression. That a major general should hold this post may seem odd, but Pakistan was functioning under a martial law system, where all key administrative posts were held by the military.[6]

As of 1971, the Pakistani armed and security forces deployed in East Pakistan consisted of four types of formations:

- regular armed forces of Pakistan (Army, Air Force and Navy)
- border guards
- paramilitary formations
- police

The sole Pakistan Army formation originally deployed in East Pakistan was the 14th Division, the four brigades of which were established between 1963 and 1970 and were almost completely staffed by West Pakistanis. Its build-up is summarised in Table 3. As of 1971, the HQ of 14th Division controlled a total of 18 battalions (i.e. equivalent to two divisions), four field artillery and one anti-aircraft battalions, plus a single tank battalion (consisting of five squadrons with a total of 50 M24 Chafee light tanks).[7]

Table 3: Build-up of the 14th Division, Pakistan Army, 1971

Year	Establishment of Elements
1963	53rd Brigade (Comilla) and 107th Brigade (Jessore)
1964	57th Brigade (Dacca)
unknown	23rd Brigade (Rangpur)

As well as the ground forces of its regular Army and paramilitary units, the East Pakistani garrison included No. 14 Squadron, PAF, with 16 North American F-86E Sabre fighter-bombers, one

Ironically, while India was a main export customer for Soviet-made equipment, the USSR donated several Mi-8Ts to Pakistan, thus equipping it with a more powerful helicopter than the Mil Mi-4, the standard assault and transport type in IAF service. This Mi-8T, one of four examples operated by the Pakistan Army in East Pakistan, is seen unloading relief supplies in mid-1971. (Albert Grandolini Collection)

Of course, the few available Pakistani Mi-8Ts were mainly used in support of the Pakistan ground forces. This example (serial 1024) was caught on camera while transporting a light artillery piece. (Albert Grandolini Collection)

Lockheed T-33A, four Aérospatiale SE.316B Alouette IIIs and four Mil Mi-8 helicopters.[8] The Pakistanis also operated several riverine craft and gunboats (all inter-provincial communication was run via the rivers of East Pakistan).

Because it was mainly composed of Punjabis, who were happy to adopt British theories about 'martial races', the Pakistan Army was insistent on converting this bias into a tradition. Therefore, the PA converted only two pioneer battalions staffed by Bengalis into infantry, in 1948: only about 50 percent of their officers and 10 percent of their other ranks were Bengalis. Thus came into being the East Bengal Regiment (EBR). By 1971, a nominal total of nine battalions were established, several of which were still in the process of working up, and two were deployed in West Pakistan, as listed in Table 4. Even as of that year, their total complement was a mere 6,000.[9]

Table 4: Battalions of the East Bengal Regiment, 1948–1971

Battalion	Established	Notes	After the revolt
1st	1948	Fought in Lahore sector during the 1965 India–Pakistan War, mutinied at Jessore in March 1971, fled to India, subsequently became known as 'Senior Tigers'	Re-established in India June 1971
2nd	1948	Mutinied at Joyedpur 19 March, escaped to India, became known as 'Junior Tigers'	Re-established in India June 1971
3rd		Mutinied at Rangpur, fought the PA before escaping to India, became known as 'Mini Tigers'	Re-established in India June 1971
4th	1965	Sole all-Bengali battalion of the PA, mutinied at Comilla, fled to India, became known as 'Baby Tigers'	Re-established in India June 1971
5th	1966–69	Deployed in West Pakistan, fought in Ajnala sector (Punjab)[10]	Remained in West Pakistan as of June 1971
6th	1966–69	Deployed in West Pakistan with 18th Division PA, taken into custody, became known as 'Lucky Tigers'	Remained in West Pakistan as of June 1971
7th	Circa 1969–70	Integrated into the PA as the 44th FFR	Remained in West Pakistan as of June 1971
8th	Circa 1969–70	Mutinied at Chittagong, fought Pakistan Army until it had to escape to India	Re-established in India Sept 1971
9th	Circa 1970	Forming, disbanded after revolt began	Re-established in India Sept 1971
10th	1970	School (Training) battalion, disarmed and sent home after the revolt	Re-established in India, date unknown
11th	1971		Established in India 1971

The border guards came into being in the form of the East Pakistan Rifles (EPR), a lightly armed border-security organisation about 12,000–15,000. Much more numerous was the 45,000–50,000 strong paramilitary *Razakars*, which in turn consisted of two types of formations: *Mujahids*, armed with obsolete rifles and guns and *Ansaris*, who were armed only with machetes and spears. From the point of view of the GHQ in Rawalpindi, what was most important was that the *Razakars* were almost entirely composed of 'loyal' elements: almost all the Mujahids were *Biharis* (Muslims who had migrated to Bengal before and after partition), while *Ansaris* were mainly Biharis, but also included a few Bengalis (who, of course, defected to a man as soon as the uprising erupted). Furthermore, the 34,000-strong police force – which almost completely consisted of Bengalis and was already showing strong ethno-political bias in 1970 – was considered unreliable.

Troops of the East Bengal Rifles before the war of 1971. (Albert Grandolini Collection)

Members of one of the *Razakar* formations, a paramilitary organisation whose troops were armed with little more than machetes and spears. (Albert Grandolini Collection)

Lieutenant General Niazi inspecting a group of *Mujahid* militiamen in mid-1971. Lack of equipment and armament, including even uniforms and boots, and Niazi's facial expression speak volumes about the condition of the defences of East Pakistan at this time. (Albert Grandolini Collection)

Pakistani Strategic Planning

Totalling some 70,000 men, the above-mentioned forces might have been enough to maintain control over East Pakistan but were hopelessly too few to fight an Indian invasion – even more so if the garrison was blockaded from the air and the sea. Thus, it must be concluded that Pakistan had no plan: if there was one, at the strategic level, it was to run offensives into Kashmir and Punjab in the West, thus distracting India from the East, and hoping for help from abroad. Gains in Kashmir would then be kept (because Pakistan claimed all of Kashmir), while other acquisitions were to be traded off for any losses in East Pakistan. This enthusiastic assumption turned out to be a major cause for East Pakistan's call for secession immediately after the 1965 war: the Bengalis realised that they were, essentially, left without protection.

At the tactical level, Pakistan's plans for the defence of the East were essentially unchanged in concept since 1967–70, when the plan for Operation Sundarbans came into being. In 1970, this was reconceptualised in a series of exercises called Titu Mir. All plans envisaged India attacking in the West while holding in the East. Major General Rao Farman Ali Khan had served in Dacca since 1967, first as commander of the 14th Division's artillery brigade and then as political advisor to the martial law commander. Perhaps presciently, he asked permission to develop a plan where India would attack in East Pakistan and defensively hold the West. That was the basis for Operation Sundarbans, as nearly as can be discovered, followed by Operation Titu Mir.[11] Consequently, forces of the 14th Division were to stage a fighting withdrawal from the border into the so-called 'Dacca bowl' – a *de-facto* island between three major rivers – and hold out there for three weeks. It was assumed that by that time Pakistan would have defeated Indian forces in the West and manage to attract international support. With hindsight, this might appear unrealistic, but once again, it should not be forgotten that the expectation was that China would hold down 10 Indian mountain divisions, and only two or at most three of the best Indian divisions would deploy against East Pakistan. Since it was assumed the population would resist India, three weeks was probably a reasonable estimate. The unrealistic part was assuming that Pakistan in the West could defeat India in three weeks, especially given India's superiority in air and naval power.

As the emergency erupted in 1971, the Pakistan Army GHQ bolstered the defences of East Pakistan through the addition of the 9th Division, supposedly the best unit of this size in its entire armed forces. Subsequently, and unhelpfully, the GHQ continued making promises for further reinforcements – which it could not send. For example, it promised to send three medium tank regiments and a squadron of Chinese-made Shenyang F-6 fighter-bombers. All of this was simply unfeasible. The solution was to avoid cracking down on the Bengalis and stall them through negotiations for at least 18 months, while building up additional units. For example, if Pakistan's 35th and 37th Divisions, raised in November 1971, had been built up and sent to the East in 1972, the local headquarters would have five fully deployed divisions, and thus an excellent chance of defeating an Indian invasion. However, instead of any such realism, the GHQ in Islamabad did something unconscionable by repeatedly promising reinforcements and aid from China and the USA, which never arrived.[12]

Table 5: Military Sectors of East Pakistan and Build-up of PA Divisions, March–November 1971[13]

Sector	Division	HQ/Operational Area
North-west	16th Division	HQ Rangpur; with 23rd Brigade (Rangpur), 34th Brigade (Bogra-Natore), 205th Brigade
North-east	14th Division	HQ Sylhet; with 27th Brigade (Mymensingh); 57th Brigade (Dacca), 107th Brigade (Jessore)
Central	36th Division	HQ Dacca; ad-hoc/paper unit
South-east	39th Division	HQ Chittagong; ad-hoc/paper unit
South-west	9th Division	HQ Jessore; with 53rd Brigade (Chittagong), 117th Brigade (Comilla), 313th Brigade (Sylhet)

Meanwhile, the plan for the Operation Titu Mir was reviewed in June 1971, but because no further reinforcements were available, it remained unchanged. It had become clear by now that the main Indian attack would come from the east, with a secondary assault from the west, while the prospects for the north-west and north-east were unclear. In July 1971, Niazi and his staff did develop plans for several offensive operations toward Calcutta, the Siliguri Corridor, and Assam, all designed to pre-empt an Indian attack, but while Lieutenant General Niazi was very keen and was backed up by officers such as the Special Service Group's (SSG) commander (who wanted to attack the Farakka Barrage across the Ganga River in West Bengal, 18km from the East Pakistan border), nothing happened in order to avoid providing India with an excuse for an intervention.[14]

Pakistan Army's Tactical Problem

The Prussian military theorist Clausewitz said: "So the defensive form of war is not a simple shield, but a shield made up of well-directed blows." The defence is the stronger form of war, but the offense is the decisive form. An army goes on the defence solely to prepare the way for the counter-offense. If a static tactical deployment is adopted, with all available troops deployed in a thin line without reserves and without lateral mobility, the enemy is left free to decide where to concentrate to break through. Once a breakthrough occurs, since there are no reserves and, in this case, no lateral mobility, the defender is left with the choice of standing fast as the enemy runs rampant in the rear, or of falling back, which means giving up territory. The standard solution to this is to launch strong counterattacks, forcing the enemy to stop and even to retreat to protect against itself being enveloped. During its war with India in 1971, Pakistan could at most times spare a platoon or a company only by weakening other parts of the line. Sending a battalion or a brigade to reinforce elsewhere was out of the question.

As of 1971, Pakistan had no reserves. An average commander needs one unit in reserve for every two deployed frontally: the reserve is intended only to buy time for preparing the counterattack. With 30 battalions covering approximately 4,000km of front along the borders of East Pakistan, from day one the 'game' for Pakistan was a losing proposition. Theoretically, this need not be, because fire can be used to cover gaps, employing air power or artillery: however, Pakistan had no firepower to spare. The feeble five or six (sources are unclear) field regiments with 25-pdrs (88mm) and four heavy mortar batteries supporting a force of five divisions could never suffice. Moreover, fire is used to slow down the enemy until reserves can be shifted to close a breach: the US used the firebase strategy successfully in Vietnam. This strategy usually worked, because the firebases were sufficiently manned to hold off attackers until helicopters and air strikes arrived. Even then, if the weather was bad, firebases were overrun (of course, the enemy paid the price once the weather improved). Given the extension of the front lines, the Pakistani reserves would have to be air-mobile. However, the PA and the PAF could only deploy eight helicopters – for an area of about 150,000 square kilometres, and in the absence of air superiority. Unsurprisingly, these had to be used with extreme caution. Similarly, the provision of just five squadrons equipped with a total of about 50 operational M24 Chaffee light tanks as support for five divisions could only be described as a symbolic gesture.

Three Plans for the Defence of East Pakistan

The defence of East Pakistan could be based on an outer ring (i.e., the border of East Pakistan), a middle ring or an inner ring, based on the Dacca bowl. The outer ring option required a thin deployment on a 3,000km front, with big gaps in the line. The middle ring could be based on the Madhumati River in the western

Indian Army gunners man a 25-pdr. Famous from the Second World War, this 88mm gun remained in widespread service in many armies around the world, well into the 1970s. The Pakistan Army had five or six field artillery regiments entirely equipped with such pieces deployed in East Pakistan in 1971. (Albert Grandolini Collection)

sector, the Meghna River in the west, and south of Rajshahi in the north. The frontages per battalion would have fallen by half, and Pakistan would have the chance to put a couple of brigades in reserve. The inner ring aimed to defend only the Dacca bowl, based on the rivers Jamuna in the west, Brahmaputra in the north and the Meghna in the east.[15]

Even an amateur strategist could tell that given Pakistan had only three real divisions deployed in the East, the inner ring was the most suitable, with a full division (or at least two brigades) as reserve. A professional strategist would prefer to start by holding the middle ring, then stage a fighting withdrawal into the Dacca bowl. For political reasons, however, Pakistan chose to hold the outer ring, with an aspirational plan to fall back slowly on the middle and then the inner rings. No exercises were held to determine the feasibility and likely problems with such a course of action, nor was there any actual rehearsal. For this, blame must fall on GHQ in Rawalpindi and Lieutenant General Niazi, General Officer Commanding (GOC) of III Corps (or Eastern Command). Pakistan had six months to carry out paper and actual exercises, ample time to be thoroughly prepared. It surpasses belief why this was not done. The reality was, however, that hardly any general believed in his mission. Had Tikka Khan, the Military Governor of East Pakistan and commander of Eastern Command until August, been left in command, it is likely that meticulously planned and executed exercises would have been conducted, because he was a through, hard-working professional. Incidentally, for those inclined to believe Tikka was 'just a butcher', once the crackdown on the rebel Bengalis (Operation Searchlight) had been conducted (and on the advice of his political advisor), he announced an amnesty, only to be overruled by the GHQ. The Pakistan Army senior command was hardly a monolith: many senior officers – both military and civil – believed that no military solution was possible, while many others did not want to see their future careers ruined by voicing opposition to GHQ's ill-conceived orders. How could Pakistan win or even force a stalemate against the Indians, given the province had a population of 75 million and Pakistan had only 46,000 regular troops, plus 70,000 militiamen, mujahids, Frontier Corps troops and Rangers (border policing troops) combined?

The US-made M20A1 anti-tank rocket launcher was the primary means of anti-tank defence of the Pakistan Army's infantry units in 1971. (Albert Grandolini Collection)

Dismal state of Pakistani Defences

In 1972, the former CO of 14th Division, Fazal Muqeem Khan, wrote an invaluable analysis of the 1971 war, focused on East Pakistan. The first insider's account from the Pakistani side, it painted a dismal picture of the state of the Pakistan Army's units deployed there, making the following points:

- The Eastern Command was woefully under-resourced.
- Troops had been fighting for six to eight months without relief. Though F.M. Khan does not say so, with PA forces spread in small packets throughout the country, clearly no unit and formation training was possible.
- Pakistan had no counter to Indian propaganda depicting Pakistani troops as mass murderers; this left them further demoralised. To worsen matters, Yahya Khan did not visit East Pakistan once after the outbreak of the civil war; troops did not even get to see their theatre commander once the war began.
- There was no plan from GHQ, which shrugged of responsibility, with the C-in-C saying it was up to the local commander to make his plans. End-state objectives were not laid out.
- Much of the PA was still US-equipped, but there had been no spares/supplies since 1965.
- In 1965, the PA had been small but highly trained and well-equipped. The post-1965 expansion left much of the army half-trained; 20 percent of officers and other ranks had no more than six months of training. Many units were raised from reservists as late as October and November 1971.
- The loss of Bengali officers and men was keenly felt at all levels, quite apart from the problem of Bengali officers deserting to the Indian Army right through the December war.

The Pakistanis were worn out from eight months of COIN (counterinsurgency) operations and had not been able to maintain field training, and were short of technical specialists, which tended to be of Bengali origin. GHQ deceived Pakistan Eastern Command by telling it that the Chinese would arrive at any moment. Once no help arrived, Pakistani morale – never high to begin with – collapsed. Moreover, the Pakistanis thought they would be allowed to evacuate East Pakistan, so why should they fight to the last? Another key factor was the massive corruption in the Pakistan Army leadership culture, which gnawed at its insides for years. Major A.H. Amin, an iconoclast and expert on Pakistan military history, has told the author of many Pakistani officers who refused to relinquish their high standard of morals and professionalism, but were consequently, almost without exception, punished by being sidelined.

Niazi as a General

Before discussing the war, it is worth studying the limitations of Lieutenant General Niazi. The intent is not to denounce or diminish him, only to explain why the Pakistani GHQ might have done better to leave Tikka Khan as commander in the East, and to highlight GHQ's faults leading to the successful secession of East Pakistan.[16]

Tikka was a capable and decisive general, tough and very determined as a combat soldier and leader. He earned himself a bad reputation by commanding the ruthless crackdown against East Bengalis; even West Pakistanis were aghast, leading to his recall. In pure COIN terms, and in the spirit of Machiavelli – who advised his prince that if something bad was to be done, to do it as quickly as possible – Tikka was right. In the Baluch insurgency of 1974–76, he succeeded in defeating the rebels, largely because there were no journalists around to report the misdeeds of his troops, committed on his orders. After transferring back from Dacca, he was given command of Pakistan's main strike force in the 1971 war, II Corps, comprising the 1st Armoured and 7th and 33rd Infantry Divisions. Indeed, he was eventually appointed the Chief of Staff of the PA, served his civilian master Bhutto faithfully and retired quietly. This was the measure of this man. Aside from the crackdown, he was not well liked because he was considered a blockhead with a one-track mind – which is, to be honest, what a country wants from its generals when it is in a tough spot.

On the other hand, Niazi was fond of the finer things of life, including good food, good wine and fast women. In typical South Asian style, everything was always the fault of someone else; he was passive-aggressive, an adherent of the school of 'I had to comply when my superiors told me to do such and such stupid thing'; and, to be fair, his orders were abnormally stupid. Still, he missed the point of being a combat commander, which is that one must do everything to convince one's own superiors they are on the right track; and, if they do not see that, to resign one's command. It is true that the top brass never once came to visit Dacca after the start of trouble. But neither did Niazi go to Rawalpindi to bully everyone, including his chief, into doing the right thing. Perhaps he did not know what the right thing was.

When writing his memoirs, Niazi raised several valid points, including:

- His orders were contradictory. India should have been held at the border, but the GHQ refused to provide the resources necessary. It is true Pakistan did not have resources, but the GHQ should have thought of that and acted in timely fashion.
- In November 1971, already too late, the GHQ promised the crack 111th Brigade and eight additional battalions to hold Dacca and strengthen weak points. Instead, it sent only five battalions. That any were sent was foolish, because this weakened Pakistan's chance of getting a countervailing victory in the West, while making no difference to the outcome in the East. Niazi was wrong in assuming the 111th Brigade was kept for a coup: it was needed for an attack on Jammu. Moreover, against whom was that unit to stage a coup? Yahya was the army commander, and if he wanted the brigade sent to the East, it would have gone. While 12 extra battalions to add to Pakistan's 30 in the theatre would have greatly slowed down the Indian advance, that would have left 12 battalions less for the West and might have led to problems there.
- The GHQ did not make artillery, armour and engineers available as needed. This is correct. The reason was it needed the heavy equipment of the 9th and 16th Divisions to form the 17th and 33rd Divisions.
- President Yahya made sure he was not disturbed while he avoided the duties of his office and instead sat down to drink. He was never available to provide guidance or orders. This is absolutely correct.
- When all was lost, President Yahya shrugged off all responsibility and told Niazi it was his show – a replay of Lieutenant General Kaul's performance while commanding the IV Corps of the Indian Army during the Sino–Indian War of 1962. If it was to be Niazi's show, Yahya should have let the Pakistan Eastern Commander do the only thing that was realistic: pull all troops back into the Dacca fortress. That would have forced India to agree to a ceasefire on more favourable terms, such as permitting the evacuation of troops instead of surrender.

Lieutenant General Niazi chatting with one of his subordinates before the war. (Albert Grandolini Collection)

- GHQ kept saying foreign intervention was on its way, when they knew it was not. This outright lie was GHQ's responsibility.
- GHQ refused to permit Niazi to enter Indian territory when necessary to defeat the insurgents or Indian Army troops. This is true, and was quite odd once India was at war with Pakistan.

That all the above was true does not make Niazi's claims of 'brilliant leadership ruined by the GHQ' true. It was not brilliant leadership to vanish among his dancing girls, wine, song and poetry after India launched its attack. A surprisingly ungenerous and petty statement made by Niazi in his memoirs shows the true measure of the man: he claimed to have exploited the Indian Army, which had "poor leadership, weak planning and [an] overcautious approach and was always doing the obvious". He also complained that Indian Eastern Command commander Jagjit Singh Aurora did not have the gambler's touch, nor did he urge his formations "to push forward at speed". This is akin to the defeated boxer telling the victor: "You failed because you could have knocked me out in round five, whereas you took till round eight." It is a strange thing to say about a victorious general; moreover, it gives no credit to his own junior officers and men who delayed the Indians, putting up a staunch defence till the last.

Many Indian commanders were cautious because that is the way they were trained and they were heedful of their men's lives. Moreover, several Indian generals put in bold and aggressive performances, particularly Jack Farj Rafael Jacob, Alok Singh Kler, Gandharv Nagra and Sagat Singh, plus numerous flag officers in IV Corps. The Indian Army's level of improvisation at division, brigade and battalion level was also impressive.

CHAPTER 3
THE PRE-WAR WAR

One crucial question when discussing the 1971 Indo-Pakistani War is: when did that conflict really start? Already in 1971, in a master propaganda stroke, India had successfully convinced the world that the war was provoked and began with the Pakistani 'pre-emptive' air strike on forward air bases of the IAF in the west, on 3 December 1971. For its own reasons, Pakistan was happy to follow in similar fashion, and an amazing number of histories of this conflict published in the West ever since loyally repeat this legend even half a century later. The mass of histories of the Indo-Pakistani War of 1971 ignore a series of dramatic – and tragic – developments in East Pakistan that year. The period between the Pakistan Army's crackdown upon not only the political opposition in that province, but indeed its population, and the 'official' start of the war on 3 December 1971 is frequently given little attention, although the period from March–October 1971 was of crucial importance to the flow of the conflict. This is particularly surprising considering that regular Indian Army units were deployed inside East Pakistan as early as October 1971, and a full-scale invasion began on 21 and 22 November. The feeble Pakistan air strikes on IAF air bases in the west during the late afternoon of 3 December were originally planned to be launched in reaction to a general Indian offensive expected for 1 December, pushed back to 2 December and then postponed to the 3rd. There is only anecdotal evidence for Pakistani claims that India began laying down artillery fire on 3 December: there is, however, solid evidence that two days earlier, Prime Minister Indira Gandhi cancelled the planned western offensive on the behest of the USSR (an episode that will be covered in Volume 2 of this book). What is crucial is that India had invaded East Pakistan already on 21 November 1971, and – under valid international laws – Pakistan had every right to hit back, whether in the East or in the West. That Islamabad decided not to do so was largely related to its reluctance to fight a two-front war against a vastly superior opponent.

Indian Prime Minister Indira Gandhi in 1967. (Official release)

Blood and Thunder

As indicated above, affairs in East Pakistan were already out of control well before 3 December 1971. Indeed, the showdown began even before the December 1970 elections – and during the following 12 months, enough happened to validate its own, separate volume.

Following months-long tensions, in February 1971, East Pakistan exploded into a general strike and mass demonstrations, the central point of which was independence. When Lieutenant General Tikka Khan arrived in Dacca to take over as a newly appointed Martial Law Administrator later that month, he found the province paralysed. All the usual municipal amenities had ceased to function, food supplies for the units of the Pakistan Army were cut off, their movement hindered, and armed insurgents were assassinating officers and non-commissioned officers (NCOs). At that point, Sheikh Mujibar Rahman was the *de-facto* ruler of East Bengal, his Awami League having taken over the administration – not only because of its landslide victory, but because the Bengalis constituted the majority of civilian administrators and the police – but he cautiously refused to announce this, even when addressing over one million of his supporters in Dacca on 7 March 1971. One might expect that Sheikh Mujibar would have already attempted to establish links to the Bengali officers of the EBR. However, there is no indication he did so before 19 March, when he contacted – the meanwhile retired – Colonel Muhammad Ataul Goni Osmany, the officer crucial for the establishment of the East Bengali Regiment. By then it was too late, as the PA was already in the process of rendering leading Bengali personnel ineffective: they were sent out on purposeless missions or disarmed on flimsy pretexts. Nevertheless, several mutinies of EBR troops erupted, during which many officers of the PA were murdered (eventually, the Bengalis killed all 700 Pakistani officers of the EBR). The mutineers subsequently ran away, taking their arms with them. Meanwhile, civilians began organising armed resistance on their own, and a large number of armed insurgent movements began attacking the Pakistan Army troops.

Eventually, civil disobedience, harassment, assassinations and mutinies by Bengali troops prompted Tikka Khan to request permission to "crush them in 48 hours", which was granted by Islamabad. While Tikka and his staff were developing plans, the PA redeployed the 13th Frontier Force and 22nd Baluch by Lockheed C-130 Hercules transports of the PAF and airliners of the Pakistan International Airlines (PIA), from West Pakistan to the East, and then began distributing 9,000 tonnes of ammunition and supplies brought to Chittagong aboard the MV *Swat*. Concurrently, local loyalists – mainly Islamists – were organised into paramilitary movements such as Razkars, al-Badr and al-Shams, all kept under Army control. On 24 and 25 March, a group of generals toured major garrisons by helicopter to personally brief commanders on Operation Blitz. Subsequently renamed Operation Searchlight, and objected against by the Governor of East Pakistan, Vice-Admiral Syed Mohammad Ahsan, this was run under tight security and aimed to disarm the six regiments and training centre of the Bengali-staffed East Bengal Regiment and secure control over six major urban centres. As happens in any guerrilla war, many armed organisations subsequently emerged.

Operation Blitz/Searchlight

Launched on 25 March 1971, Operation Searchlight proved a success and was largely concluded in a matter of two weeks. The PA was a well-trained, all-volunteer, long-service organisation, capable of simultaneously sacking the civilian administration and much of that of the EBR, while attacking most police posts and murdering their occupants *en masse*. Though the application of shock tactics and harshness to quickly end a revolt was hardly an invention of the Pakistan Army, the ferocity with which it acted was unanticipated. Worse still, right from the start, the military operation either included or provoked extensive mass murder. Apparently on his own initiative, but with the knowledge and approval of the brigade commander, the CO of the 53rd Field Regiment not only sacked and disarmed the entire 4th East Bengal Regiment, the 40th Field Ambulance and Bengali members of the SSG at Comilla: he ordered all 17 officers and 915 other ranks shot. As described by Brigadier Karrar Ali Amin, then in command of a paramilitary formation stationed near Chittagong, the prisoners were brought out to the squash court in groups and executed, with the next group forced to bury the bodies in a ditch dug by a bulldozer, before being executed in turn. Meanwhile, Karrar was told to bring his non-Bengali troops and their families into the cantonment for their safety. Instead, he disarmed his Bengali

The winner of the December 1970 election, and leader of the Awami League, Sheikh Mujibar Rehman, at a press conference before the crisis of 1971. (Albert Grandolini Collection)

troops and let them go: while these fled over the border to India, he returned to the garrison with 80 men and their families.

Almost simultaneously, the Bengalis began mass killings of Biharis and Hindus (the latter having been a target of multiple pogroms since 1940). While all that President Yahya Khan wanted was for the Pakistan Army to crush the disorder – and he was right to do so under the UN Charter – the situation spiralled out of control. The Biharis joined the Pakistan Army in acts of retaliation. The Hindus of East Pakistan, who at that time constituted 30 percent of the province's population, thus found themselves attacked from three sides: by the Bengalis, the Biharis and the PA. In all too many instances, ethnic and religious hatred was less of a cause than economics, many simply grabbing Hindu land and looting their assets. Also, poor as India was, East Bengal was considerably poorer. For many Biharis and Bengalis, flight to India thus promised a better life. Unsurprisingly, refugees flowing into India accelerated to 60,000 a day, possibly one of the biggest Third World refugee movements ever experienced. The Indians had anticipated a refugee flow and had made preparations but were overwhelmed by the vast numbers that kept arriving.

With hindsight, one can conclude that there was no need for any of these dreadful acts. The Bengali soldiers could have been simply disarmed and interned. After all, any Bengali troops stationed in West Pakistan were disarmed and imprisoned, or segregated and watched, but none were executed. However, contrary to the popular narrative, the PA did not launch Operation Blitz/Searchlight with the intention of a genocide. The truth is that its commanders lost control, because of the earlier assassination of their comrades and because their troops felt frightened and left on their own. They knew they were caught in the middle of 75 million people who wanted to kill them. Relatively few Pakistani soldiers believed that if enough Bengalis were murdered, the rest would be forced into obedience. Perhaps surprisingly, the Pakistani Army readily admitted to massacres: it did not claim innocence in the matter, though figures of three million Bengalis killed and 300,000 women raped have long since been discredited. However, once the crackdown began, Bengalis became open about killing all regular and irregular members of the armed forces and their supporters, Biharis and Hindus. In an absolute moral sense, the Pakistan Army did wrong, no matter what wrong was done to them. That is the theory, yet the reality was different. For the Bengalis, the West Pakistanis were the enemy, but what was the Bengali excuse to kill Biharis and Hindus? A clear answer to this question remains unavailable, just like the number of their victims.

Pakistan Army troops detain students in Dacca on 25 March 1971. (Albert Grandolini Collection)

A squad of Pakistan Army troops prepare for a patrol during counterinsurgency operations in April 1971. (Albert Grandolini Collection)

Bengali Forces

Although a Bengali insurgency was already visible by mid-March 1971, the planners of Operation Blitz/Searchlight never expected prolonged Bengali resistance. Early reports about small-scale armed resistance – notably at Iqbal Hall, Dacca University and the Rajarbagh Police HQ, from 25 March – were ignored, and the Bengalis could thus quickly assemble about 10,000 trained men into what they called the Mukti Fouj in some places, and Bangladesh Army in others. Units consisting of professional soldiers put up a strong fight. For example, Major Zia-ur-Rahman of the 8th Battalion EBR, with six officers and about 200 troops, took control of much of Chittagong,

Students of the University of Dacca were some of the first to take up arms and offer resistance to Operation Blitz/Searchlight. While highly enthusiastic – and said to have been one of the best-educated insurgencies ever – they were too poorly armed to stand any serious chance of success in a confrontation with troops of regular Pakistan Army units. (Albert Grandolini Collection)

In reaction to Operation Blitz/Searchlight, the nascent Bengali insurgency reacted with widespread sabotage actions, which severely disrupted nearly all road and rail communications in East Pakistan. (Albert Grandolini Collection)

The Pakistan Army's campaign against separatists in East Pakistan was a merciless operation of extermination. Tragically, it provoked fierce retaliation: these four captured PA troops were summarily executed by the Bengali insurgents. (Albert Grandolini Collection)

including the local radio station, on 25 March. Two days later, he was able to broadcast a call for the people to take up arms against the Pakistanis. Zia's group resisted several counterattacks until being forced to withdraw from the city on 30 March, eventually making their way to India. Elsewhere, the insurgency launched a large number of devastating sabotage operations, with road and rail communications disrupted, bridges blown up and rivercraft sunk. Led by junior officers – because most senior officers were either imprisoned or killed in cold blood by the Pakistanis – the insurgency then made a mistake by taking on PA units head-on. In mid-April, it began fighting for control of several towns. Although scoring some early successes, this effort turned into a costly failure. The Pakistani forces were well-entrenched in their cantonments, usually located at a distance from the towns and cities: indeed, their concentration in northern and western East Pakistan made the rebels' survival nearly impossible. However, elsewhere, the emboldened insurgents felt strong enough to try occupying entire sections of towns. Forced into the realisation that they were fighting a semi-conventional war, the Pakistani forces rallied in strength and hit back with everything available. In the course of pitched battles, they destroyed much of the resistance, forcing the survivors to flee over the border to India. This should have been a worrisome development for both Niazi and the GHQ in Rawalpindi, because they had to expect that the insurgency would now receive support from New Delhi. However, this was not the case.

Bangladesh Army

While the initial Bengali armed resistance to the Pakistan Army's crackdown was spontaneous and disorganised, as the civil war in East Pakistan heated up through April, thousands, then hundreds of thousands of Bengali civilians followed the fleeing survivors of the EBR and insurgency to find refuge beyond the country's western, northern and eastern frontiers. The leading Indian intelligence agency, the Research and Analysis Wing (RAW), had maintained contacts with the rebellious Bengalis – including their leader Sheikh Mujib Rahman – for many years. Although Mujib was arrested and transferred to Pakistan to stand trial in late March, his aides remained loyal and their organisation maintained its cohesiveness. Thus, instead of wasting time with nonsense about factionalism and infighting, the RAW was quick in reorganising the exiled Bengalis. The importance of this factor – especially a united rebel front – cannot be overemphasised. While all of eastern Bengal was already shut down before the Pakistan Army was able to re-establish control, a provisional government of Bangladesh came into being on 17 April 1971 in the Meherpur district of western East Pakistan. Moreover, Colonel M.A.G. Osmani – the 'father of the EBR' – was with the officers that escaped to India. He was soon followed by dozens of others and was appointed the head of the emerging Bangladesh Army. Over the following months, Osmani found himself in at least nominal command of around 80,000–90,000 highly motivated guerrillas, reorganised and trained by the Indian Army.[2]

Between April and October 1971, India thus organised a large native insurgent force and a regular armed force, plus a replacement government, that not only provided a good excuse for a military intervention, but to which power could be handed over on the day of any ceasefire, without any requirement for a troublesome and cost-intensive transitional period or for Indian forces to remain once the war was over.

Mukti Bahini

Meanwhile, and despite the severe losses in April, the armed uprising inside East Pakistan went on under the name of the 'Freedom Fighters' (Mukti Bahini, MBs). To what degree the uprising continued is signified by the fact that no less than three million Bangladeshi citizens claimed to have served with the movement. It took 48 years for the Bangladesh Government to give the true figure: 210,000. The Bahinis claimed an epic and heroic role for themselves in the civil war, with colourful and exaggerated accounts. The struggle has been raised to sacred proportions by the people of Bangladesh, and for decades their claims were accepted at face value. Without intending to denigrate anyone, the claim there were 15 fighters for every actual one shows the degree of inflation.[3]

Regardless what they professed for themselves, or what the Pakistanis thought about them, Indian historians do acknowledge the MB's contribution. The Indian Army knew the real situation, but diplomatically chose to remain quiet: it was genuinely upset with the pressure put on it to turn out a barely functional guerrilla movement in huge numbers, while preferring a much smaller, yet more effective force. The confusion about the effectiveness of the East Bengali insurgents was further increased by the incorrect use of the term Mukti Bahini for *all* insurgents that fought against Pakistan's armed forces from early March 1971, when armed groups were organised by students in the form of the Mukti Faui. When and where exactly the first of them was created, or when were they renamed the Mukti Bahini, remains unclear, but it is certain that both designations generically referred to the people who fought in the Bangladesh Liberation War. The cold truth is that the irregulars contributed to a degree that is impossible to quantify. In late March 1971, the original cadre of students was reinforced by officers and other ranks that defected from the Pakistani armed forces. Many of them were subsequently provided with eight months of additional training by the Indian Army. While never meant nor expected to become frontline infantry, they were deployed to supplement Indian Army units and acquitted themselves well. After the war, they formed the core of the Armed Forces of Bangladesh. The second type of MBs were Indian Army troops mixed with Bengali guerrillas, trained to run commando operations in the Pakistani rear, exploiting their excellent knowledge of local circumstances, combined with the expertise of Indian troops. The third category consisted of students, farmers and workers, many of them leftists, given just two-to-four weeks of training on firearms. There was no way for them to prove combat effective, but they did create a 'sea' in which the Pakistani armed forces had to swim. While only occasionally managing to pick up a few Pakistani soldiers, or blow up some culvert, their effect upon enemy morale was indisputable.

Colonel Osmani, the 'father of the EBR' and later the first commander of the Bangladesh Army. (Albert Grandolini Collection)

Bengali refugees undergoing training on a Czechoslovak-made ZB 1937 machine gun in India. (Albert Grandolini Collection)

A group of Mukti Bahini in typical dinghy boats during a commando operation inside East Pakistan during the second half of 1971. (Albert Grandolini Collection)

The mass murder of separatists and the Bengali intelligentsia during Operation Blitz/Searchlight left the members of the Pakistani armed forces – like the three regular and several irregular troops visible in this photograph – swimming in a sea of literally millions of hostile Bengalis. (Albert Grandolini Collection)

Kaderi Bahini and Others

The third largest and certainly the most self-publicised of the Bengali insurgent movements was the Kaderi Bahini, set up by a former Pakistani Army volunteer who left before the outbreak of war. He is said to have created a 17,000-strong force that completely controlled five districts along the 101st Communication Zone's line of advance. The founder of this force, Kader Siddique, adopted the glamorous sobriquet of Tiger Siddique. He claimed to have fought 73 engagements with the Pakistan Army, was successful in all and lost 36 of his combatants killed in action. Even the most superficial forensic analysis shows that there is no manner in which anyone could have fought so many engagements and lost just one KIA for every two fights. Here, it suffices to say that Tiger did help the men of the 2nd Parachute Regiment of the Indian Army during the assault on Tangail – to collect their equipment and regroup for their next move on the road to Dacca. Tiger was supposed to accompany the Indians, but he did not: he only arrived in time to bravely bayonet disarmed and restrained prisoners and others he had rounded up, in full view of the press. Perhaps he impressed his countrymen, but otherwise earned the disgust of the Indian Army and besmirched Bangladesh's name throughout the world. Where the photographers were, Kader was also to be found. There is a famous picture of him looking dashing and hand-feeding sweets to Mujib Rehman, the Bangladeshi political leader, when the latter was set free by Pakistan after the ceasefire. This is a celebratory ritual in South Asia. When the surrender was being signed, Kader was also present. The Indian RAW and Army also established a 4,000-strong force that was kept secret even from the Bangladeshi military leaders, intended to provide close protection for Mujib against the multiple competing militias (many of whom were communist). That said, the RAW and the

---

Voyage of the East Pakistan Rifles

A good example of what the Bengali officers and other ranks went through during the traumatic months of March and April 1971 is offered by Rafiqui Islam. Born in Naora, near Chandpur in East Pakistan, Islam graduated from the Pakistan Military Academy in Kakul in 1963 and was commissioned as a lieutenant with the Engineering Corps in 1965, before shifting to the Artillery Corps and then being transferred to East Pakistan in 1968. As of 1971, he wore the rank of a captain and was assigned to the 8th Battalion of the East Pakistan Rifles.

On 24 March 1971, Islam found out that the Pakistan Army was about to deploy reinforcements by sea and air. Expecting the worst, he decided to alert fellow officers and other ranks of the East Pakistan Rifles in the Chittagong area, convincing them to defect and disarm troops holding multiple border posts in that part of East Pakistan. The same day, the merchant ship MV *Soyat* had arrived in Chittagong and began unloading arms and ammunition for the 57th Brigade of the Pakistan Army. Islam and his comrades protested in the centre of the city, only to come under attack from the 20th Battalion of the Baluch Regiment, during which several Bengalis were killed. This incident sparked the defection of some 7,000 officers and other ranks of the East Bengal Rifles, and to them organising armed resistance. Initially at least, the rebels were most successful in the Chittagong area. Commanded by Major Ziaur Rahman, members of the East Bengal Rifles arrested and disarmed every loyal PA officer they could lay their hands upon, and then organised defence positions in Kalurghat. It was from the local radio station that the Bangladeshi Declaration of Independence was broadcast by Ziaur Rahman and M.A. Hannan, on behalf of Sheikh Mujibur Rahman. Unsurprisingly, the Mukti Bahini movement led by Rahman and Islam was easily overpowered during the counterattack of the Pakistan Army in April 1971 and forced to flee to India. Rahman was subsequently assigned the command of Sector-1, which stretched from Chittagong Hill to the Muhiri River in the eastern side of Noakhali district, before taking over as commander of Z-Force (also known as the 'Tura Brigade') on 10 June 1971. After assuming command of Sector-1, Islam led attacks by naval commandos that sunk several Pakistani barges during Operation Jackpot in August 1971. Subsequently, he led the Mukti Bahini advance on Chittagong, which successfully concluded on 15 December 1971. Islam was the first to enter the Circuit House, lower the Pakistani flag and replace it with the flag of Bangladesh. Although rising in rank to major after the war, Islam eventually turned to politics and later served in the government of Sheikh Hasina.

Indian Army helped create several communist militias, too. This may seem peculiar, but there was a logic to it. In a civil war, multiple competing factions arise. If they were not kept under control, the end of the anti-Pakistan insurgency could have seen serious infighting: this was an ideal way to co-opt fractious militias.

Table 6: Major Bengali Insurgent Factions, 1971

Movement	Notes
Bangladesh Army/ Niamoti Bhani	80,000–90,000; initially defectors/mutineers from the EBR; reorganised, reinforced and retrained in India; formed the core of the Bangladesh Army from 1972 onwards
Mukti Bahini	250,000, mostly civilians; emerged from Mukti Faui, originally formed by highly motivated villagers and students
Latif Mirza Bahini	8,000–10,000 civilians from Sriajganj and Rajshahi
Kaderi Bahini	17,000 civilians; established 1 March 1971 in Tangail zone, led by Kader 'Tiger' Siddique
Mujib Bahini/ Bangladesh Liberation Force (BLF)	4,000 civilians, mostly students, members of the Awami League, organised, equipped and trained by the Indian Army and the RAW; reportedly never fought in the war; subsequently merged into the paramilitary Jatiya Rakkhi Bahini
Hemayet Bahini	2 ex-Pakistan Army NCOs and about 5,000 irregulars active in Faridpur area
Akbar Hossain Bahini	800 irregulars active in the Jhinajdah area
Quddus Molla & Gafur Bahini	Irregular group active in the Barisal area

Highly enthusiastic, even if poorly equipped and lacking heavy weapons early on, once the different Bengali insurgent movements began receiving arms, training and guidance from India, they were to prove their mettle in combat during the final months of the war. This photograph shows a column carrying ammunition and supplies. (Albert Grandolini Collection)

The enthusiastic support of the Bengali population – for the insurgents and for Indian Army troops – knew almost no limits: even youngsters willingly provided help by carrying ammunition and supplies around the battlefield. (Albert Grandolini Collection)

Kilo Flight

The Bangladesh Army included plenty of former officers and other ranks of the Pakistan Air Force. By July 1971, a total of nine pilots and 58 ground personnel led by Group Captain A.K. Khondakar came together. In the course of the suitably codenamed Operation Jackpot, the Indians provided them with aircraft, helicopters and other supplies. The result was the establishment of Kilo Flight – the predecessor of the Bangladesh Air Force – on 28 September 1971. This was a unit commanded by Squadron Leader Sultan Mahmud that, after two months of training, consisted of 17 officers and 50 technicians, and was equipped with one Douglas DC-3 Dakota, one de Havilland Canada DHC-3 Otter and one Aérospatiale SE.316B Alouette III helicopter. Operating from Dimanpur airfield (constructed during the Second World War), Kilo Flight was to fly its first combat operations during the evening of 3 December 1971.

The sole DHC-3 Otter of Kilo Flight was this example, painted olive drab on top surfaces and sides, and wearing the Bangladesh national insignia and the yellow serial 8721 on the fuselage sides. Between 3 and 16 December, aircraft and helicopters of Kilo Flight flew a total of 40 combat sorties against ground targets in Sylhet, Comilla, Daudkandi and Nashigndi, and one – unsuccessful – search and rescue sortie for a downed IAF fighter-bomber pilot. (Albert Grandolini Collection)

The only Alouette III of the Mukti Bahini's Kilo Flight. Note in the right foreground a launcher for 2.75-in. (68mm) unguided rockets, and a twin machine gun inside the cabin. Like the solitary Otter, it was deployed for hit-and-run attacks on Pakistani Army positions by night, to avoid PAF interceptors. (Albert Grandolini Collection)

Stages 1, 2, and 3

Ultimately, India's involvement in the 1971 war in East Pakistan – also known as the Liberation War of Bangladesh, or Bangladesh War of Independence – can be described as going through at least seven phases, as follows:

1. April–May: receive, shelter and start training the armed resistance.
2. May–October: infiltration, sabotage and establishment of permanent strongholds inside East Pakistan by insurgents, Indian Army regulars and Indian border troops; deep reconnaissance; build up logistic base for offensive, and remedy shortages of equipment and ordnance.
3. October–November: brigade and division training; increasing penetration by battalion-sized units of regular and border troops.
4. November: launch a wholesale pushback of Pakistan Army deployed along the border.
5. 22 November–3 December: covert brigade-sized attacks on multiple axes.
6. 3–16 December: all-out, open attacks to encircle and destroy Pakistan Army.
7. Seizure of Dacca.

Though seven stages have been demarcated, there were considerable overlaps between them and, obviously, New Delhi's strategy developed gradually. Initially, until the end of May 1971, the plan was to train Bengali combatants to seize a strip of territory around East Pakistan, permitting the declaration of an independent Bangladesh and shifting their provisional capital from Calcutta to the liberated area. The new government would appeal to India, the UN and other foreign powers for help – which India was ready to provide. But the Bengalis' means never matched their needs, and in engagement after engagement, the rebels came out worse than the PA. Consequently, it became unavoidable that mixed groups of Indian Army regulars and insurgents would join the fighting. These events can be compared to the Vietnam War during the period of 1963–65, when a number of fighters described as South Vietnamese were actually highly trained regulars of the North Vietnamese Army. Unsurprisingly, New Delhi incessantly talked about the "achievements of the Mukti Bahini" – and not without good reason, for by November 1971, the Indian-controlled Bengali insurgents were organised as listed below in Table 7.

Table 7: Organisation of Indian-supported Bengali Forces

Movement	Composition	Notes
Bangladesh Army (Regular Forces)		
Z Force	1st, 3rd, 8th Battalions EBR	each with own light artillery battery
K Force	4th, 9th, 10th Battalions EBR	each with own light artillery battery
S Force	2nd, 11th Battalion EBR	each with own light artillery battery
1st Mujib Field Battery		est. Aug 1971, 4 x 3.7-in. mountain howitzers
2nd Field Battery		est. Oct 1971, 6 x 105mm mountain howitzers (Italian-made)
3rd Field Battery		Est. Nov 1971, 6 x 105mm mountain howitzers
Kilo Flight (Air Force)	1 helicopter, 1 DHC-3, 1 DC-3	
Navy		550, mostly commandos
Sector Forces (Paramilitary Forces)		
Sector I		HQ Harina; Chittagong District, eastern Noakhali District; COs Major Ziaur Rahman (Apr–June 1971), Major Rafiqul Islam (June 1971 – Feb 1972)
Sector II		Districts of Dacca, Comilla, Faridpur and part of Noakhali; COs Major Khaled Mosharraf (April– Sept 1971), Major A.T.M. Haider (Sept 1971 – Dec 1972)
Sector III		Between Chauraman Kathi and Sylhet District in the north, and Singerbil to Brahmanbaria District in the south; COs Major K.M. Shafiullah (Apr–July 1971), Captain A.N.M. Nuruzzaman (July 1971 – Feb 1972)
Sector IV		HQ Karimganj, later Masimpur; from Habigani District in the north to Kanaighat Police Station in the south; COs Major Chittarajan Datta (Apr 1971 – Feb 1972), Captain A. Rab (period unknown)
Sector V		HQ Banshtala; Sylhet
Sector VI		HQ Burimari (Patgram); Rangpur District and part of Dinajpur District; CO Wing Commander M. Khademul Bashar (Apr 1971 – Feb 1972)
Sector VII		HQ Taranngapur; Rajshahi, Pabna, Bogra and part of Dinajpur Districts; COs Major Nazmul Haq (Apr–Aug 1971), Major Kazi Nuruzzaman (Aug 1971 – Feb 1972), Major A. Rab (period unknown)
Sector VIII		HQ Benapole; Kushtia, Jessore, Khulna, Barisal, Faridpur and Patuakhali Districts; from May 1971 Kushtia, Jessore, Khulna, and northern Faridkot Districts; COs Major Abu Osman Chowdhury (Apr–July 1971), Major M.A. Manzur (Aug 1971 – Feb 1972)
Sector IX		Barisal, Patuakhali and parts of Khulna and Faridpur Districts; COs Major M.A. Jalil (July–Dec 1971), Major M.A. Manzur (period unknown), Major Joynal Abedin (period unknown)
Sector X		naval commandos only
Sector XI		HQ Teldhala, then Mahendragani; Mymensingh and Tangail Districts, parts of Rangpur, Gaibandha, Ulipur Upazila, Kamalpur and Chilmari Upazila Districts; COs Major Ziaur Rahman (June–Oct 1971), Major Abu Taher (Oct–Nov 1971), Squadron Leader M. Hamidullah Khan (Nov 1971 – Feb 1972)

Provision of Indian support resulted in the emergence of large groups of Bengali insurgents armed with the India-made 9mm 1A1 sub-machine gun carbine – a licensed version of the British-designed Sterling L2A3 sub-machine gun – two of which are visible in this photograph. (Albert Grandolini Collection)

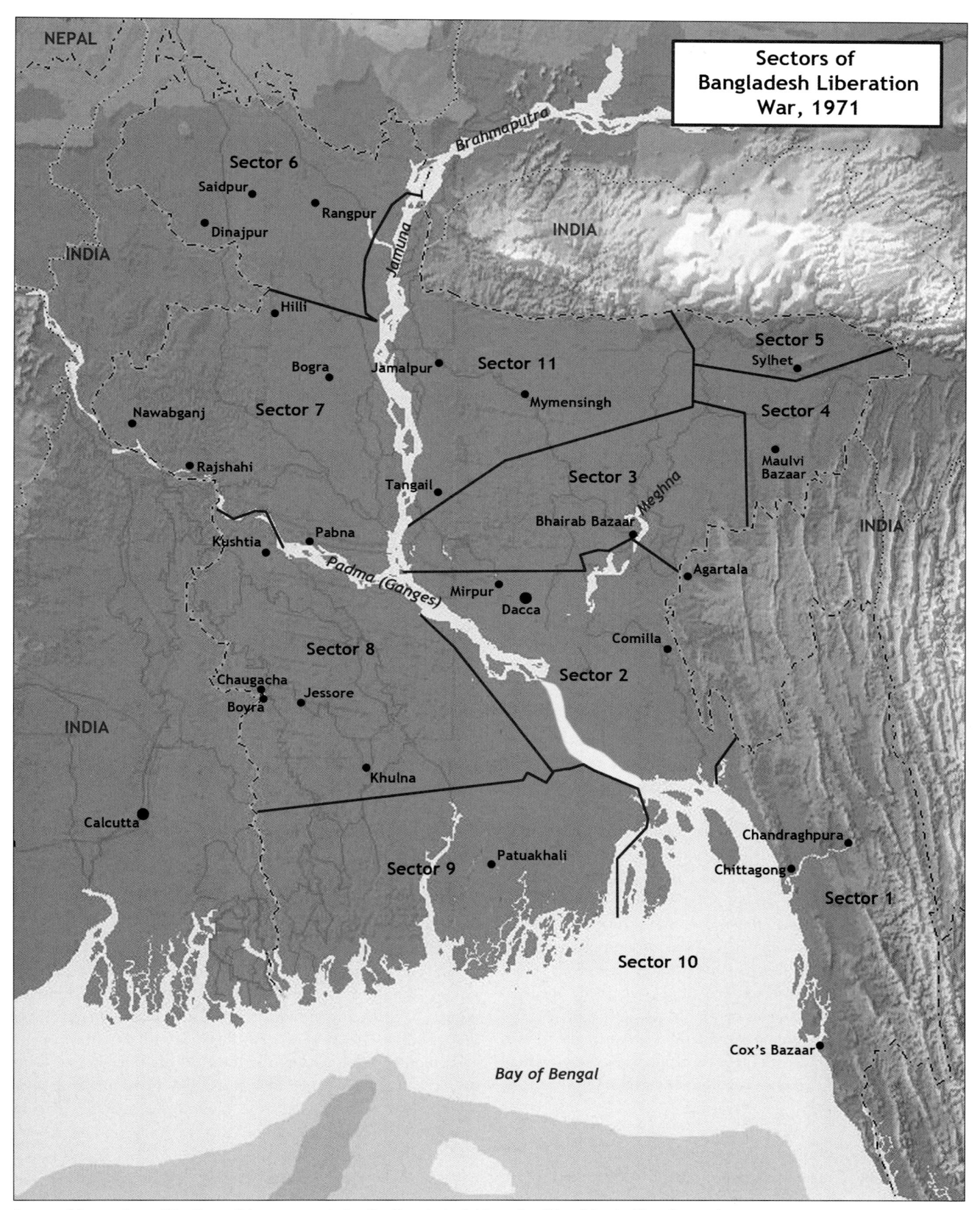

A map of the sectors of the Bengali insurgency during the Bangladesh Liberation War. (Map by Tom Cooper)

The longer the crisis in East Pakistan went on, the better-equipped Mukti Bahini units began to appear. This group was not only armed with an interesting assortment of bolt-action rifles, but with assault rifles and light machine guns; some of its combatants even received helmets captured from the Pakistani Army. (Albert Grandolini Collection)

Planning the Intervention

The initial idea for an Indian military intervention became known as the 'Subramanyam Option', the essence of which was to strike with elements of the Indian armed forces already on hand – preferably before Pakistan could build up its defences. This found no support among the Indian Army's commanders. The British Indian Army had fought like Montgomery: a slow but steady build-up, rigorous training and acclimatisation, and then a massive advance when everything was in its favour. Moreover, the Indian Army was very concerned about the possibility of a Chinese counter-invasion to help Pakistan. Thus, shifting troops from their Himalayan garrisons had to be put off to the last minute; it was only in October that the process began, and India decided on overt war to coincide with the first snows in the India–Tibet passes, which would limit Chinese intervention capability. Equally, the Indian Army was concerned that Pakistan might launch a pre-emptive war from West Pakistan. While Indian armoured forces were well trained, equipment deficiencies had to be made up and the formations shifted to the west from central and southern India. As a general rule, India's military readiness was low – to save money. In such a situation, the commander of the Indian Army, General Manekshaw, was simply not about to take the risk of hastily attacking East Pakistan. His remit was further complicated by standing orders that survived from 1947: no ground was to be lost, anywhere. This unsound policy made it impossible to wage a war designed to get results. It was one reason why in 1947–48 and again in 1965 the Indian Army appeared to make no progress: generals could not take any risks. And of course, when an army attempts to defend everywhere, it will win nowhere. The Pakistanis, on the other hand, were always willing to leave one sector or another uncovered to mass somewhere else.

Dacca Plan

The next plan that surfaced at the GHQ in New Delhi called for the seizing of territory in Bangladesh to first declare an independent Bangladesh that would invite India to help the new country by sending in troops, and then resettle refugees that had fled to India.

Accordingly, the Indian Army's XXXIII Corps would seize a 100km front stretching from Jalpaiguri in the north-west through Bogra. The II Corps – especially raised for the war in East Pakistan in September 1971 – would then exert pressure against Bangladesh's western border by seizing territory west of the line Kushtia–Khulna, focusing on Jessore and keeping Pakistani forces tied up and unable to reinforce the north-west. Headquartered in Tezpur, the IV Corps would defend the border in the east to prevent Pakistan from shifting troops to the north-west and to protect against a Pakistani counteroffensive from this direction. Should this plan not work, IV Corps was to seize the Chittagong area in south-east Bangladesh in support of Border Security Force units and Uban Force operating in the Chittagong Hill Tracts south of the Lalmai Hills to fulfil the two objectives.

By seizing the ports of Chittagong and Khulna, General Manekshaw thought that Dacca would automatically fall as East Pakistan would be cut off from resupply. The Chief-of-Staff of Eastern Command Indian Army, Major General Jack Farj Rafael Jacob, was aghast:[4] since the Indian Navy was to blockade East Pakistan, why was there a need to focus on Khulna and Chittagong? A possible reason is that while the three Indian services coordinated better than at any time in the past, this was not a truly theatre-wide coordination, and Manekshaw did not see Khulna and Chittagong ports as irrelevant.

One way or another, this plan was the one with which India began the war on 21/22 November 1971, and which converted the military intervention into something of an overkill. But what was to be done about Dacca, Bangladesh's political, economic, cultural, military and communications centre? The nominal objective of every war is to capture the focal point (or centre of gravity), causing the collapse of peripheral forces and ending the war in short order.

Ironically, and regardless of assertions by several well-informed Indian historians, Dacca was not an objective for the Indian Army. One reason for this was that India assumed retreating Pakistan forces would fall back to Dacca, which would probably result in messy and lengthy fighting in an urban area, causing delays and heavy Indian casualties. Another reason may have been that going for the capital would shred the already weak pretence that Bengali rebels were doing the fighting, with only restricted logistic help from India.

But why did India feel time-constrained? The Army HQ laid down a 21-day plan, after which it was assumed – reasonably – that UN or foreign intervention would take place. The rebels had failed from the start, even with Indian help, and there was no way for them to defeat three divisions of tough Pakistani regulars. Furthermore, India believed it could not attack before December 1971. There was no logistics infrastructure in the east; months were required to build roads, increase capacity of the few metre-gauge rail lines and make up shortages for all three services. And the ground did not start drying out until October. Then the Tibet passes would be snow-blocked in December, limiting Chinese counter intervention. Manekshaw's preference was to attack in early spring 1972, but that would have given Pakistan more time to destroy the rebels. Besides, having triggered the crisis, Prime Minister Gandhi was under tremendous domestic pressure to resolve it by creating an independent Bangladesh. Lastly, the huge influx of refugees was destabilising an already unstable north-eastern India. The region was suffering from a large and expanding communist revolt (the Naxalites), in addition to moves for separatism among local tribes.

Geography and Equipment Issues

Because of East Pakistan's geography – a topic never receiving enough attention in contemporary military history – the theatre was divided into five sectors by the Pakistanis and four by the Indians. Bangladesh is slightly larger in size than the state of Ohio in the USA, and essentially consists of a low plain containing the combined deltas of the Ganges (Padma) and Brahmaptura (Jamuna) Rivers. The fertile alluvial delta region is criss-crossed by about 300 rivers and an even larger number of streams, that have created rich silt. The seaward margin of the Ganges delta, known as the Sunderbans, is intricately divided by tidal channels and covered by dense mangrove forest. The labyrinth of deltaic channels excels in producing both food and famine caused by flood and is a nightmare for conventional military operations. While the land in the delta is seldom more than 50 metres (about 150ft) above sea level, high ground can be found on the fringes of the area, such as in the Barind in the north-west, the upper Surma valley in the north and the Chittagong Hill Tracts in the extreme south-east. However, the higher areas are poorly populated. In between numerous rivers and canals are *bils* – marshes – some enormous in size and permanently retaining water, while others dry up with the seasons. The monsoon covers the period from early June to early October and extends from the Bay of Bengal towards the north and west. July is the rainiest month; there is often a break in August, and then minor breaks in October, followed by storms that frequently increase humidity to more than 80 percent. The climate is moderately warm for eight months of the year, with considerable humidity and heavy summer rainfall that produce an enervating effect on human life and cause a high incidence of sickness. Malaria is prevalent all over the land.

Most transport to this day is riverine. In 1971, there was little inter-sector movement possible as the transport infrastructure was limited, and what existed had been seriously damaged by Bangladeshi forces working under Indian command through mid-1971.[5]

The Indian Army eventually deployed in the theatre included the 6th Division. Normally deployed in northern Uttar Pradesh, this unit could not move without permission from GHQ, and was to immediately shift to Bhutan in the case of a Chinese attack there. Similarly, the Eastern Command of the Indian Army kept its 17th and 27th Divisions in place in Sikkim, and the 2nd and 5th Divisions in Arunachal Pradesh. Thus, about half the Indian forces usually deployed along the Chinese frontier were redeployed for the war in East Pakistan, and so consisted of troops that, at last initially, were not acclimatised. Fortunately for India, the growing crisis prompted the GHQ in New Delhi to start moving these forces – and then the 4th, 9th and 20th Divisions – closer to the future battlefield quite early, and thus very few formations – except some independent brigades and the 6th Division – needed to be inducted into the theatre once battle was joined.[6]

Nevertheless, before going into action, the Indian armed forces still had to solve several other serious issues. Although in possession of stocks for 60 days of combat operations, many critical items were available only for 10 days. MiG-21 interceptors, for example, were in large-scale production by Hindustan Aeronautics Limited (HAL), and in operational service, but the IAF was still short of spares for them. Similarly, the number of available drop tanks for Sukhoi Su-7BMK fighter-bombers was to prove hopelessly too small. The 8th and 57th Divisions had yet to be prepared for taking part in combat operations. Most seriously of all, units withdrawn from the frontier with China still needed about two months of retraining and were lacking bridging equipment, wheeled transport and firepower: at their usual positions high in the Himalayas, they needed no pontoon bridges, while the bulk of their artillery consisted of US-made 75mm and Yugoslav-made 76mm guns, and 120mm mortars, and much of their ammunition was not interchangeable. Finally, not only could the infrastructure in India not possibly support a deployment of the equivalent of nine divisions – with the number of available roads, bridges and railway lines having to be significantly expanded – but because of the monsoon season, East Pakistan in October 1971 was comparable to a giant swamp. Any movement of heavy equipment, or of a large number of motorised vehicles, was extremely difficult, made more so because much of the local infrastructure had already been destroyed by the insurgency in order to deny mobility to Pakistani forces. Even once the monsoon was over, so many culverts were destroyed – either by Indian forces or the withdrawing Pakistanis – that Indian Army troops repeatedly had to stop their advance, while bypassing them was impossible due to the amount of standing water.

The Indian Army also had only around 70 percent of the field grade officers needed. Although training of additional cadets was accelerated (and compressed from 12 to four months), the shortage was such that many officers had to be withdrawn from air defence formations, reserve infantry battalions or other supplementary units. More often than not, these officers proved unsuitable for their new tasks and front-line combat units refused to accept them, while many deserted.

Indian Commanders

Having known both personally, my information on Lieutenant General J.S. Aurora, Commander of the Indian Army, and Major General J.F.R. Jacob, Chief-of-Staff, Eastern Command Indian Army, is neither second-hand nor impressionistic. General Aurora was a smartly turned-out, easy-going officer and disinclined to break with the consensus or disobey orders. Jacob was intellectual, raffish, proud of his Jewish heritage and attracted to high risk. Which is not to say he was reckless; he was professional and steady, but also ambitious and determined to make a name for himself. He was not modest about his abilities. He lacked a high opinion of many of his seniors and colleagues; but as shown by his memoir of the Bangladesh war, he was generous with his praise for competent officers who got the job done without the non-stop negativity and endless pessimism for why something could not be done. This is a deeply ingrained Indian characteristic, one of the many reasons why India has fulfilled its potential in the world.

Major General Jacob, later during his career. (official release)

Brigadier (later Major-General) H.S.Kler, CO 95 Mountain Brigade (left), and Major-General G.C. Nagra, CO 101st Communication Zone (centre). The other officers are unknown.

Jacob wrote his memoir 26 years after the war and had ample time to think over what he wrote.[7] As mentioned above, when he asked Eastern Command to release his papers, he found they had been destroyed because some junior functionary did not want a record to survive of India's help to East Pakistan rebels. This is just another example of the reverence with which Indians treat their history. In reading his memoir, the lack of original records must be kept in mind. He was essentially relying on his memory. And he certainly was not shy about taking credit for his achievements, but there is nothing wrong with that.

Jacob makes it clear there was no Indian plan to do more than seize a belt along the Indo–East Pakistan border, allowing Bangladesh to declare independence.[8] He is also very clear that the Army, at least, had zero intention of advancing to Dacca. Since the Army does what the Government tells it, a reasonable surmise is that New Delhi did not want to overrun East Pakistan for a multiplicity of reasons. However, as early as April 1971, Jacob and his staff prepared plans for an advance to the provincial capital. While no one accepted the plans, Jacob did what every good officer should do: he ignored his superiors and kept planning and giving orders as if Dacca was the objective. Many of his corps and division commanders did not think the objective was realistic, and said so, but Jacob bulldozed on. He acted so confidently that no one guessed that neither GOC Eastern Command, nor the Chief of Army Staff, were aware of what and his staff were up to.

Soon enough, both the GOC Eastern Command, his superior, and the Army Chief found out what Jacob was really after, and he got a dressing down. Wholly unembarrassed, he told GOC Eastern Command that this was all approved at the highest level and he was told to keep it secret. The easy-going GOC let the matter go.[9]

It was under these conditions that the Eastern Command achieved all its original objectives – plus advances beyond – by 2 December 1971. When Pakistan then made a lukewarm attempt to pre-empt in the West – where the Indian attack was postponed at least once on Mrs Gandhi's orders – hawks like General Jacob had the excuse they wanted, while the Prime Minister quickly rubber-stamped the advance to Dacca.[10]

CHAPTER 4
THE ROLE OF FOREIGN POWERS

As well as India, three external powers became involved in the Indo–Pakistan War of 1971, and each of them played their own role, at least indirectly influencing the developments on the front lines between Islamabad, New Delhi and Dacca.

Soviet Position

In the wider public, it is generally considered as a 'given' that during the Indo–Pakistani War of 1971, the USSR provided wholehearted support only for India. Ironically, all authoritative sources agree that the Soviet position regarding this conflict was actually even-handed.[1] There is no doubt that Moscow had become involved in India in the 1950s, when providing significant economic aid. By 1962, the Soviets were supplying helicopters and transport aircraft. By the mid-1960s, US President Lyndon B. Johnson was so fed-up and angry with India, and its never-ending appeals for aid without reciprocation, that he wanted nothing to do with the 1965 war. When the Soviets saw their opportunity to step in, Johnson was just as happy to leave the problem of South Asia to them. That war thus ended with a ceasefire arranged through Soviet mediation at Tashkent. It was a disaster for India, but a disaster of Indian doing, and not Moscow's fault. Full of Gandhian forgiveness and graciousness toward the enemy, the Indian Prime Minister – who was also a Gandhian – was persuaded by his advisors to return Indian gains in Kashmir in exchange for the usual rhetoric from Pakistan about peace and cooperation. The negative consequences of this give-away reverberate to this day, but that is another story.

From the Soviet point of view, the next logical step was to consolidate the hold on South Asia and undercut US influence through negotiating cooperation between India, Pakistan and Afghanistan. The Soviets also wanted the three countries to be part of the containment of China. This move eventually went nowhere, but Moscow worked hard to be even-handed between India and Pakistan, supplying economic assistance to the latter and even weapons. Though the amounts were probably in the range of what they sent to India in six months, the Indians were not pleased and the Soviets had to back off somewhat. Most amusingly, at the same time the Soviet arms and spares continued flowing into Pakistan – even once the civil war in East Pakistan was in full swing in May 1971.[2]

Did India loudly denounce the Soviets' two-faced behaviour? Of course not! Indian 'non-alignment' meant bashing the US at every step while being tolerant of the USSR, and while publicly 'exposing' what New Delhi called 'American transgressions' at every opportunity, in the Soviet case no disputes were ever publicised. The hypocrisy is hard to take. Moscow's perceived need to be even-handed between India and Pakistan explains why, when the Pakistan civil war flared up, it took a neutral position and did not condemn Pakistan. As the East Pakistan situation deteriorated, Moscow was delighted when Prime Minister Gandhi asked to sign a friendship treaty – for which the Soviets had been pushing for two years – and only then did the USSR turn against Pakistan. The reason was opportunistic: Islamabad finally realised it could not wean Pakistan away from the USA and China, while Moscow quickly concluded that a secession of Pakistan was unavoidable. This is why the Soviets finally went 'all in' for India, to a degree where they managed to manipulate New Delhi into leaving West Pakistan after the war: after all, from their point of view, the fall of West Pakistan would only complicate relations with the USA at the time that China was opening up, and negotiations for the Strategic Arms Limitation Treaty (SALT) were more important than keeping India happy. Finally, Pakistan was supportive for the Arab case in the Arab–Israeli conflict, and thus Moscow was not ready to give up on it. Consequently, Soviet diplomats in New Delhi ended playing a flawless game in 1971: instead of operating on ideology, they went for immediate gains. Even though Soviet diplomacy was populated by highly educated, mostly brilliant, professionals with long-term experience in their areas, they thus acted unusually for this era. While certainly having their internal – and tough – debates over this issue, they knew what they were talking about, and they were quick to decide and act. They showed a refreshing pragmatism in advancing their nation's interests, eschewing ideology and following realpolitik.

US Position

By contrast, the administration of US President Richard B. Nixon chose to side with the party it knew would lose. Even though they anticipated Bengali independence from the start, Nixon had strange ideas of how China would react if he abandoned Yahya, and had an even more curious idea of sticking by his man through stormy and calm seas. Not to mention his pure hatred of Mrs Gandhi. However, a president of the USA is not supposed to get emotional over such things, and Nixon was perfectly capable of cold-blooded action. Even as he was standing by Yahya because he liked him – never asking what Pakistan had ever done for the US (zero, just like India) – he was preparing to sell-out South Vietnam because his larger plans required him to leave Indochina. Even with the US media, public, Congress and foreign service against Yahya, Nixon was doing his brave Dutch boy act of plugging with his finger Yahya's failing dyke. It is one thing to be a complex personality; it's quite another to act against *your own country's interest*.

US President Nixon (right) with Pakistan President Yahya Khan. (official release)

US President Nixon (right) with Bhutto in 1973. (official release)

PR China's Position

As a Pakistani ally, China did not want to see Pakistan broken up. But its options in coercing India were severely limited. In 1962, China was able to throw eight or nine divisions against India's three brigades deployed on the frontier with Tibet. Because of the very tough terrain in the Central Sector, and the Indians deploying a full division there, China left this area alone: the People's Liberation Army's commanders did not like such odds. Instead, they put a division against a single Indian brigade protecting a no less than 400km stretch in the Ladakh area, three divisions against a single brigade in western NEFA (North East Frontier Agency), and a reinforced division against a single brigade in eastern NEFA. They prepared carefully for months, including inducting some of their best divisions from eastern China. Not by launching 'human wave' attacks, as widely claimed, but through deployment and good combination of superior manpower, firepower and tactics, the Chinese defeated three Indian brigades.

In 1971, however, China was still severely suffering because of the Cultural Revolution which ripped the country apart. Mao Tse Tung and his enemies were locked in a mortal succession struggle. The army was equally riven and was functioning as an internal security force to bring the Red Guards under control, while the economy had all but collapsed. Moreover, the Indian frontier was now protected by 11 powerful mountain divisions, significantly stronger than their Chinese counterparts; the IAF, meanwhile, had 40 fighter squadrons and was ready for action, unlike 1962, when New Delhi had been afraid to use its airpower. India now had all the bases and forward air landing grounds (for logistical support) it needed. Indeed, the 1967 clash in the Sikkim sector saw many Chinese casualties and demonstrated a burning Indian desire to avenge the 1962 defeat. Under the circumstances, Beijing wisely confined itself to moral support and arms for Pakistan.

CHAPTER 5
AIR AND NAVAL WARFARE

At a first look, it might seem that air power and naval warfare played only minor roles during the 1971 war in East Pakistan. In a grand overview like that provided in this volume, this impression might appear to be confirmed due to the relatively few reports about spectacular, major operations by air and naval forces. However, both air and naval power played a crucial role because of the geographic separation between West and East Pakistan.

Indian Navy's Task Forces

During the run-up to the war, and in relation to East Pakistan, the Indian Navy was tasked as follows:

- Deploy its own naval commandos and Bangladeshi forces to run a campaign of sabotage with the aim of neutralising Pakistan's ability to use the waterways of East Pakistan (Operation Alpha).
- Blockade East Pakistan, ensuring that no reinforcements or armament could reach the Eastern Command of the Pakistani armed forces.
- Ensure that no Pakistani armed forces could escape from East Pakistan.

To run the latter two operations, the Indian Navy deployed two small task forces in the Bay of Bengal, comprising the following:

- INS (India Navy Ship) *Vikrant* (R-11) escorted by frigates INS *Brahmaputra* (F34) and INS *Beas* (F37), corvettes INS *Kamorta* (P77) and INS *Kavaratti* (P80), and the submarine INS *Khanderi* (S22).
- LST (Landing Ship Tank) *Gharial* (L3032) and LST *Guldhar* (L3033), escorted by destroyer INS *Rajput* (D141).

Displacing 16,000 tonnes at standard load, and 19,500 tonnes deep load, INS *Vikrant* was considered a 'light carrier'. Originally constructed as one of the Majestic-class light aircraft carriers for the British Royal Navy during the Second World War (as HMS *Hercules*), but never completed, it was acquired by India in 1961, outfitted and armed with 16 40mm Bofors anti-aircraft guns. While the number of anti-aircraft guns was subsequently reduced to eight, the primary armament of INS *Vikrant* became an air group consisting of British-made Hawker Sea Hawk fighter-bombers and French-made Breguet BF.1050 Alizé anti-submarine aircraft. Despite significant investment into this acquisition and related training, INS *Vikrant* originally proved of little use for the Indian Navy. Constructed in rush during the 1940s, the ship was not made to last. Indeed, it began showing its age only a few years after entering service and sat out the 1965 war with Pakistan in the port of Bombay due to internal fatigue cracks and fissures in the water drums. The crisis in East Pakistan in early 1971 prompted New Delhi into maintaining the flagship of the navy: replacement drums were acquired from Britain, enabling sea trials to be run during April 1971. These led to the conclusion that the machinery had to be operated at reduced power, decreasing the ship's top speed to 14 knots (26kmph). One way or the other, the *Vikrant* was prepared for war and embarked a total of 20 Sea Hawks from Indian Navy Air Squadron (INAS) 300, at least four Alizés of INAS 310 and two Aérospatiale SE.316B Alouette III helicopters of INAS 321.

INS *Vikrant*'s escorts included two air defence frigates: INS *Beas* and INS *Brahmaputra* both belonged to the Type-41 Leopard-class, three of which were constructed for India in Britain in the late 1950s. Each was equipped with air search radar and height-finding radar, and armed with two twin 4.5-in. (113mm) Mark 6 dual-purpose guns (mounted in turrets forward and aft), two twin 40mm Bofors guns and a single Squid anti-submarine mortar. INS *Kamorta* and INS *Kavaratti* both belonged to the Arnala-class of anti-submarine corvettes, constructed at the naval dockyard at Visakhapatnam, and based on the Petya III-class of Soviet origin. Each was armed with two twin-76mm guns, four RBS-6000 anti-submarine rocket launchers and three 533mm torpedo tubes, plus depth charges. INS *Khanderi* was a diesel-electric powered attack submarine of the Soviet Foxtrot-class, constructed in India as the Kalvari-class during the late 1960s. The boat was armed with 10 533mm tubes for a total of 22 SET-65E and SAET-60 torpedoes it could take on board.[1]

INS *Rajput* was originally constructed in Britain as the R-class HMS *Rotherham* during the Second World War. As one of the classic gun-armed destroyers of this period, it displaced 2,464 tonnes at full load and was armed with four 4.7-in. (120mm) Mark IX guns installed in single mounts, four 2-pdr (40mm) Mark VII quad-mounts, six 20mm Oerlikon guns and eight torpedo tubes. Acquired by New Delhi in 1948/49, by 1971 it was one of the oldest ships in the Indian Navy. On the contrary, the two LSTs – INS *Gharial* and LST *Guldhar* – belonged to the four newly constructed Soviet-made Polnocny-D-class landing ships (original Soviet designation Project 773U). While relatively lightly armed – each carried four launchers for 9K32 Strela-2 air defence systems (ASCC/NATO-codename SA-N-5), two 30mm AK-230 air defence guns and two 140mm Ogon 18-barrelled rocket launchers – they could actually provide substantial fire support while carrying up to 250 troops, 12 armoured personnel carriers or four main battle tanks.[2]

A top-side view of INS *Vikrant*, the first aircraft carrier of the Indian Navy. Clearly visible are seven Sea Hawk fighter-bombers parked around and opposite the island, mid-ships, and three Alizé anti-submarine aircraft on the rear of the deck. Another Alizé is on the forward part of the deck, and one more is visible on the forward elevator (seen in lowered position). (Albert Grandolini Collection)

Table 8: Naval Balance of Power, Indian Navy and Pakistan Navy, 1971

Indian Navy	Pakistan Navy
1 aircraft carrier (20 Sea Hawk, Alizé and helicopters)	None
2 cruisers	1 cruiser
4 Foxtrot-class fleet submarines	1 fleet submarine, 3 Daphne-class coastal submarines
22 destroyers and frigates	6 destroyers and frigates
8 Osa-class fast missile craft (FAC)	None
8 minesweepers	3 minesweepers
2 LSTs	None

What happened to PNS *Ghazi*?

Unsurprisingly, considering the importance of an asset such as an aircraft carrier, the first obstacle INS *Vikrant* and its escorts had to overcome – at least in theory – was a Pakistani attack submarine. What exactly happened in this regard remains a matter of heated debate to this day.

PNS (Pakistan Naval Ship) *Ghazi* (S130) was Pakistan's first submarine, obtained from the USA under a four-year lease. During the night of 3/4 December 1971, it vanished off the Indian naval base of Visakhapatnam in the Bay of Bengal. The Indian Navy claims it was depth-charged by INS *Rajput*, whereas Pakistan says it was sunk by the premature explosion of a mine it was laying off the port to sink INS *Vikrant*, or that it ran into its own minefield as it exited after laying the field. The media, which must dramatize to get the attention of readers, terms this as the greatest mystery of the 1971 war. That depends, of course, on one's point of view; there are other mysteries still unresolved.

The *Ghazi* (meaning 'Islamic holy warrior fighting against non-Muslims') in its US incarnation was the former Tench-class submarine USS *Diablo* (SS-479), named after the devilfish, and was sold to Pakistan and recommissioned in 1964. The key point is it was not conveyed as a weapon of war, but as a training boat, or for use against communist countries such as the USSR or People's Republic of China. Around the same time, India had been looking at Britain's Oberon-class submarines, but London was unwilling

INS *Vikrant* (background) with one of the Arnala-class corvettes (foreground left) and a Foxtrot-class attack submarine, during work-ups prior to the war of 1971. (Albert Grandolini Collection)

to see a then top-of-the-line boat in the hands of a nation that was not an ally. India turned to the USSR, which quickly put under construction the four above-mentioned Foxtrot-class submarines. Even though India was acquiring reasonably modern submarines from Moscow, Washington did not want to offend India by arranging modern boats for Pakistan. After acquisition, Pakistan had the *Ghazi* slightly modernised and purchased 10 mines and 14 torpedoes in Turkey. The torpedoes were Second World War relics and of doubtful reliability. Moreover, when the *Ghazi* sailed for the Bay of Bengal, several of the crew lacked the experience necessary for the safe conduct of combat operations.

The *Ghazi*'s final voyage was typical of bold but badly planned Pakistani actions. It was sent to ambush the INS *Vikrant* as the latter left port in the Bay of Bengal. However, and unknown to Pakistan, India had anticipated this very possibility and moved the carrier to the Andaman Islands. Nevertheless, the *Ghazi* proceeded to lay its mines. Several Indian naval commanders accept that the Pakistani submarine could have run into its own minefield. Other possibilities suggested by India include that there was excessive hydrogen production while recharging its batteries, or even that a torpedo launched at (most likely) INS *Rajput* circled back to blow up the *Ghazi*. What is certain is that the Indian destroyer was looking for the *Ghazi*, hoping to draw it out and sink it. The *Rajput* picked up signs of underwater movement with its sonar and released two depth charges; a loud explosion was heard, then nothing. Some Indian analysts suggest that the depth charges set off a mine laid by the *Ghazi*, which exploded and sank the submarine.

In 1972, both the USA and USSR separately offered to lift the *Ghazi*, but India declined. Indeed, New Delhi did not even send a diving team to break into the sunken boat until many years later. Moreover, India subsequently destroyed its own search and investigation records. Since India had already credited the *Rajput* with the kill, and since there was no mechanism to get records released to the public, it would seem India was hiding the truth from its own senior officers who had begun to write their memoirs and histories of the 1971 naval war. In turn, given that the *Ghazi* was in no condition for combat, the act of sending it east was rash. Yet had it damaged or sunk the Indian carrier, the Pakistani propaganda victory would have been immense. Boldness is a fine quality for commanders, but they should minimise the risks before acting rather than closing their eyes and rushing headlong and heedless into danger.

USS *Diablo* in 1964, shortly before it was sold to Pakistan. (LCDR Tomme J. Lambertson, USN)

THE INDO-PAKISTAN WAR OF 1971 VOLUME 1

Some 178 second-hand PT-76 amphibious tanks acquired by India between 1968 and 1970 played a vital role during the 1971 Indo-Pakistan War, starting with the Battle of Garibpur, fought on 20 and 21 November. During that clash, 14 PT-76s of the 45th Cavalry supported the 14th Punjab and Mukti Bahini in an attack on the village of Garibpur, an important crossroads in the Boyra salient. During the Pakistani counterattack, and in cooperation with recoilless guns, PT-76s knocked out eight M24 Chaffee light tanks of the 3rd Independent Armoured Squadron and captured another three, while losing two tanks in return. This illustration shows a typical Indian Army PT-76 during the campaign: most were left in the original dark green livery, applied before delivery, and wore a set of tactical markings applied low on the forward hull. Command vehicles also tended to receive additional markings on the turret. (Artwork by David Bocquelet)

While the majority of Indian Army PT-76s – all armed with a 76.2mm gun equipped with a variety of ammunition including HEAT (High Explosive Anti-Tank) – were left in dark green overall, at least some received a quite elaborate camouflage pattern, either in light earth, as shown here, light green or even grey. Many had their hull numbers (or registration plates) crudely overpainted with whatever colour was available. Others had tactical insignia – usually in the form of white squares or circles – applied either on the turret or on drums attached to the turret. The two examples illustrated here appear to have been assigned to the 5th Independent Armoured Squadron, supporting the 57th Division's drive on the Meghna River in eastern East Pakistan. (Artwork by David Bocquelet)

The primary means of anti-tank defence – and also of fire support – for the infantry on both sides of the 1971 Indo-Pakistan War were 106mm recoilless guns. Most were based on the US-designed M40 and installed either on Willys MB jeeps – a large number of which were in service on both sides – Indian-manufactured Mahindra Jeep CJ3s or US-made M38s. The M40 recoilless rifle was an air-cooled, breech-loaded, single-shot gun firing fixed ammunition – including HEAT, High Explosive Plastic-Tracer (HEP-T), canister or High Explosive Anti-Personnel rounds. It was equipped for direct fire only and aimed with the help of an affixed M8C .50 cal (12.7mm) spotting rifle, installed directly atop the tube, or an optical sight. (Artworks by David Bocquelet)

i

The most powerful tank deployed on the battlefields of East Pakistan in 1971 was the T-55, equipped with the 100mm D-10T rifled gun. The Indian Army deployed two major units equipped with this type – the 63rd and 69th Armoured Regiments – both on the western side of East Pakistan. In their first action, during the Battle of Garibpur on 22 November, T-55s of the 63rd Armoured Regiment knocked out three M24s of the 29th Cavalry Regiment, Pakistan Army. As far as is known, all were left in their dark green overall livery as painted before delivery, but received fake fume extractors on their gun barrels: originally, this was a measure necessary to distinguish them from Chinese-made Type-59s, based on very similar T-54s operated by the Pakistan Army. Many Indian T-55s had additional fuel drums attached on the rear of their turrets. (Artwork by David Bocquelet)

With the mass of units deployed for the intervention in East Pakistan being infantry or mountain formations, the Indian Army deployed relatively few armoured personnel carriers. The most prominent of these were Czechoslovak-designed and manufactured OT-64 SKOTs, 300 of which were acquired by India during the 1971–74 period. As far as is known, all were left in dark green overall livery, and wore a bare minimum of tactical insignia. The vehicle had 6–13mm of armour and was armed with a single 14.5mm KPV and coaxial 7.62mm PKT machine gun installed in the turret. Capable of reaching speeds up to 94kmph, the OT-64 was a very fast APC: it also had amphibious capability and could reach up to 9kmph in the water. (Artwork by David Bocquelet)

The Pakistan Army had only about 60 M24 Chaffee and a handful of PT-76 tanks deployed in East Pakistan. Initially, most were operated by the 29th Cavalry (shipped east in February 1970), which by December 1971 had its four understrength squadrons spread over 270km along the western border with India. A separate troop of four was available in the Chittagong area, but then reinforced by a few PT-76s and redeployed to the Comilla sector. Ten additional M24s found stored in Dacca were organised into the 3rd Independent Armoured Squadron and sent to the Jessore sector: this unit lost seven tanks in its first clash with Indian PT-76s, T-55s and recoilless guns on 20–21 November. Unsurprisingly, apart from the widespread use of the white strip around the turret, occasionally interrupted by white turret numbers, M24s in East Pakistan in 1971 wore relatively few markings, except for their hull registrations applied on the lower front and rear hulls. A '402' in white on a blue and yellow square applied on the right front fender may have been the tactical insignia of the 3rd Independent Armoured Squadron. (Artwork by David Bocquelet)

THE INDO-PAKISTAN WAR OF 1971 VOLUME 1

In 1971, paratroopers of the Indian Army still wore uniforms and equipment either based upon or similar to that of British paratroopers during the Second World War. This machine-gunner of the 2nd Battalion, 50th Parachute Brigade, is shown with a Mk. II paratrooper helmet (with net and scrim), a local copy of the famous 'Denison' smock and the British Model 1937 pattern webbing, in addition to the Indian Army's green overall trousers. His weapon is the famous Bren light machine gun, a dated but still reliable weapon converted to 7.62x51mm NATO standard ammunition. (Artwork by Anderson Subtil)

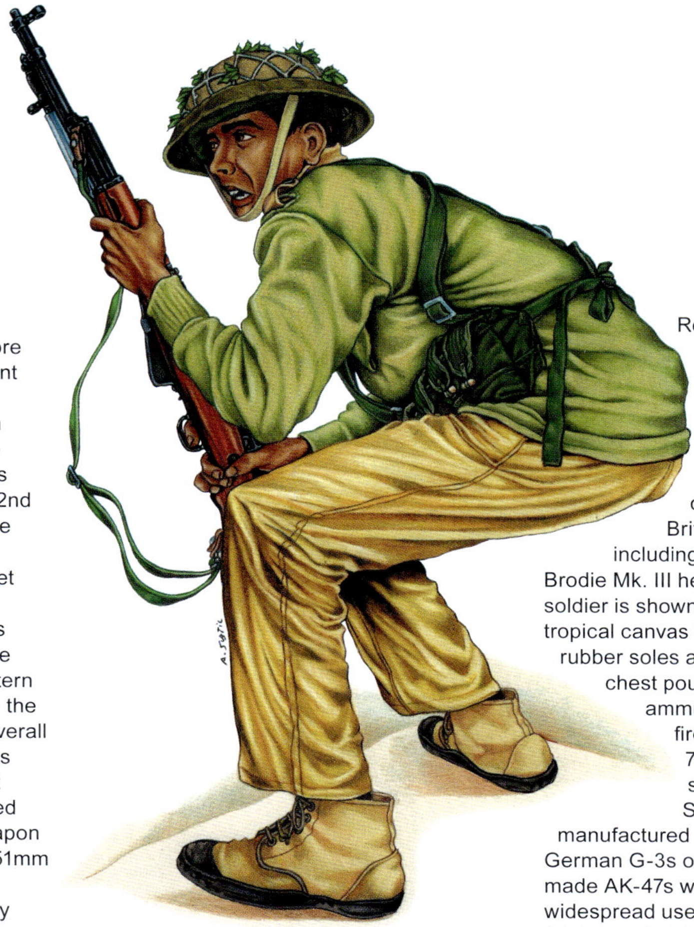

Regular Pakistan Army troops deployed in East Pakistan in 1971 wore uniforms of obvious British influence, including the classic Brodie Mk. III helmet. This soldier is shown wearing tropical canvas boots with rubber soles and 'ChiCom' chest pouches for ammunition. His firearm is the 7.62x39mm semi-automatic SKS rifle, manufactured in the USSR. German G-3s or Soviet-made AK-47s were also in widespread use. (Artwork by Anderson Subtil)

Indian Army tank crews in 1971 still predominantly used British gear and equipment. This Sikh crewman is shown wearing the common green overall jumpsuit over his uniform, and belt and suspenders from the British 1937 webbing. In place of the standard Soviet cloth and rubber helmet, he wears the traditional turban of his religion, complemented by Polaroid goggles and a leather mask for his nose and mouth. (Artwork by Anderson Subtil)

Lieutenant General Amir Abdullah Khan Niazi wearing attire in which he most often appeared in public in 1971, the standard fatigues of the Pakistan Army's officers and a black beret. Over his left breast pocket is the usual collection of ribbon bars related to his decorations, but the circular badge on the left sleeve remains unclear. His Model 1937 canvas belt is used to carry a tank crew pistol – an Enfield No.2 of .38-in. calibre. (Artwork by Anderson Subtil)

iii

ASIA@WAR VOLUME 18

As delivered from the USSR in the late 1960s and early 1970s, the mass of MiG-21FLs of the IAF were left in their original 'colour': this consisted of one layer of clear lacquer mixed with 5 percent aluminium powder, and another mixed with 10 percent aluminium powder, applied (over a layer of varnish) directly onto their metal surfaces. The resulting colour became known as 'silver grey'. Roundels were worn in six positions, and serials applied exclusively near the top of the fin. Most of the 54 aircraft deployed by Nos 4, 28 and 30 Squadrons were showing heavy wear by the end of the campaign in East Pakistan. The upper example (C1111, from No.4 Squadron, which is shown in full on the cover of this book) is illustrated as armed with a GP-9 gun-pod installed under the centreline, and an R-3S air-to-air missile under the underwing pylon. The main illustration shows C613 from No.8 Squadron, armed with FAB-500M-62 bombs: these big weapons were used by No.28 Squadron to repeatedly crater the runway of Tezgaon AB until PAF ground personnel gave up attempts to repair them. (Artworks by Tom Cooper)

Initially deployed to provide top cover for fighter-bombers targeting selected installations in the Dacca area, following a series of precise air strikes on the runway of Tezgaon AB, Indian MiG-21s were left without opposition in the air and relegated to ground strikes. This MiG-21FL C779 of No.28 Squadron was perhaps the most famous example of this variant deployed during the war in East Pakistan in 1971: it was the jet flown by Wing Commander Bishnoi in the attack on the Governor's House in Dacca on 14 December. While many other MiGs of Nos 4, 28 (crest shown inset) and 30 Squadrons received makeshift camouflage patterns in whatever dark green and dark brown colours were available, this one is shown as left in its original livery, and armed with a UB-16-57 pod for 16 57mm S-5 rockets on the underwing pylon. This jet survived the war and remained in service with the IAF for the next 30 years, mostly serving with No.8 Squadron. (Artwork by Tom Cooper)

Although four units of the IAF – Nos 15, 21, 22 and 24 Squadrons – operated Fowland Gnat F.Mk 1s over East Pakistan in 1971, there are very few photographs clearly identifying their aircraft. This example – serial E1036 – was probably assigned to No.22 Squadron, which won a decisive victory during the Battle of Boyra, after which the PAF ceased providing close support for Pakistan Army troops and, indeed, limited its activity to air defence of the Dacca area. IAF Gnats in 1971 were usually painted in the same fashion as MiG-21FLs but had a large 'anti-glare panel' in black in front of the cockpit, and dielectric surfaces painted in black. National insignia was worn in six positions. Inset is the crest of No. 22 Squadron. (Artwork by Tom Cooper)

A total of 38 Hunter F.Mk 56s and F.Mk 56As operated by Nos 7, 14, 17 and 37 Squadrons (plus five two-seaters) represented the backbone of the IAF's fighter-bomber fleet during the 1971 campaign in East Pakistan. While also armed with bombs, they flew most of their sorties armed as shown here, with four banks of three unguided rockets under each wing. This illustration shows them armed with 127mm rockets, but local variants of 80mm Swiss-made Oerlikon-Bührle Sura-D rockets might have been in use as well. The jet illustrated here was the F.Mk 56 serial BA320, from No.37 Squadron, many aircraft of which had the core of that unit's insignia (shown inset) – a black panther – applied on both sides below the cockpit. Notably, the last three of the serial were usually repeated (by hand and brush) on the cover of the front undercarriage-bay. (Artwork by Tom Cooper)

No.221 Squadron, IAF (crest shown inset), was the sole unit operating Su-7BMKs over East Pakistan during the campaign of 1971. While a big and powerful jet, the type was originally designed as a high-altitude interceptor, and thus troubled by its high fuel consumption: it proved nearly impossible to load with the required mix of ordnance and fuel. The Indians copied the Egyptian solution through mounting additional (3rd and 4th) underwing hardpoints – shown here as used for installation of UB-16-57 pods for 57mm unguided rockets – but the carriage of two 600-litre drop tanks under the centreline was always necessary in order to get them to their targets. Generally, the type was painted in the same 'silver grey' livery as MiG-21FLs, but any use of its powerful NR-30 guns resulted in massive traces of cordite down the centre fuselage and often on the drop tanks too. (Artwork by Tom Cooper)

Half of No.16 Squadron – eight aircraft in total – was the only Canberra-asset deployed by the IAF for operations over East Pakistan in 1971. They primarily flew interdiction strikes by night and at low altitude, armed with locally manufactured copies of British-designed 500lb (227kg) and 1,000lb (454kg) general purpose bombs. One of them – crewed by Flying Officer B.R.E Wilson and Flight Lieutenant R.B. Mehta – was shot down by Pakistani ground fire over Tezgaon on 15 December 1971 while flying such a mission. As far as is known, all the Canberras of No. 16 Squadron wore the standardised camouflage pattern consisting of dark sea grey (BS381C/638) and dark green (BS381C/641) on top surfaces and sides, and high-speed aluminium finish on undersurfaces. Serials (like IF919 in this case) might have been applied 'RAF-style' on lower wing surfaces but were probably removed during the war. Inset is the crest of No.16 Squadron. (Artwork by Tom Cooper)

ASIA@WAR VOLUME 18

The IAF's fleet of Fairchild C-119 Packets, provided by the USA after the Sino–Indian War of 1962, was showing its age by 1971. Nevertheless, the type saw intensive deployment during the war with Pakistan, hauling troops, supplies and equipment to a myriad of airfields close to the front lines. On 11 December, 22 aircraft of No.48 Squadron (crest shown inset) deployed the bulk of the 2nd Battalion, 50th Parachute Brigade into the famous jump at Tangail, well within the so-called 'Dacca Bowl'. As far as is known, all the involved Packets were left in bare metal overall livery but had large parts of their engine nacelles and booms painted in black. They wore national insignia in six positions, 'INDIAN AIR FORCE' titles low on the fuselage sides (in English to port, and Hindi to starboard), their serials were repeated 'RAF-style' on lower wing surfaces and they had big black code-letters (B in this case) on the forward fuselage. (Artwork by Tom Cooper)

The IAF's fleet of C-47 and DC-3 Dakotas was even more aged than that of C-119s, yet 27 aircraft from Nos 11, 43 and 49 Squadrons took place in the Tangail airdrop, even though the paras of the 2nd Battalion had never jumped from this type before. As far as is known, all were left in bare metal overall livery, but many had the top of their forward fuselage painted in white, to decrease the effects of the sun. Their serials (always prefixed by 'HJ') were applied in black above the fin-flash: many aircraft also wore the service title below the fin flash, and nearly all had code-letters in black, either applied on the rear cargo doors or directly behind these. The full serial was repeated, 'RAF-style', on lower wing surfaces. Inset is the insignia of No.11 Squadron. (Artwork by Tom Cooper)

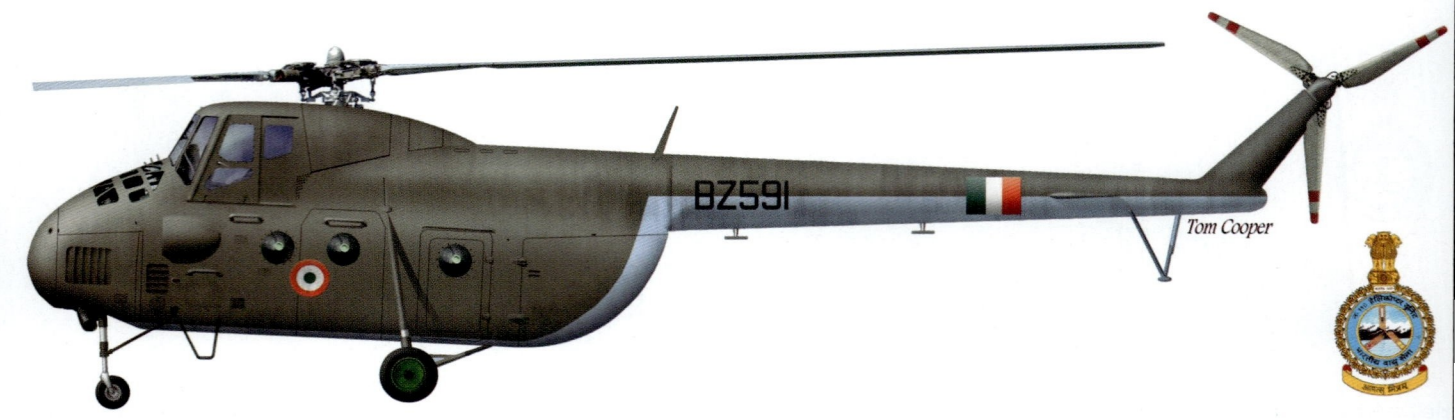

The 'heliborne workhorse' of the IAF in 1971 was the Mil Mi-4 (ASCC/NATO-codename 'Hound'). Among others, the type was used to deploy a battalion of Indian troops to the outskirts of Sylhet in the first heliborne operation of the Indian Army, and then helped take the troops of the 57th Division over the Meghna River. Sadly, very few good photographs of Mi-4s involved in 1971 have survived, but it seems that most wore the livery as shown here: olive drab (BS381C/298) on top surfaces and sides, and light admiralty grey (BS381C/697) on undersurfaces. Large serials were applied in black at the base of the boom, usually including the prefix 'BZ', while roundels were applied on the boom and the bottom of the cabin. Inset is the crest of No.110 Helicopter Unit, known to have supported the 57th Division's advance. (Artwork by Tom Cooper)

vi

The core of the air wing embarked on board INS *Vikrant* (R11) as of December 1971 consisted of Supermarine Sea Hawk FGA.Mk 6s of INAS 300. While 36 such fighter jets were acquired in the 1960s, only about 18 were still operational, but all went into action – usually armed with three unguided rockets under each wing, or alternatively with two 225kg or 250kg bombs, in addition to their four internal 20mm cannon. With one exception (an example painted black overall), all were painted in extra dark sea grey (BS381C/640) on upper surfaces and sides, and Sky S (BS381/697) on undersurfaces. Two 340-litre drop tanks were obligatory to extend their range. Inset is the crest of INAS 300. (Artwork by Tom Cooper)

Kilo Flight – the predecessor of the Bangladesh Air Force – was officially established at Dimanpur airfield on 28 September 1971, around a core of nine pilots and 58 ground personnel. It included one Aérospatiale SE.316B Alouette III helicopter, the reconstruction of which is shown here. This was painted in olive drab overall, and appears initially not to have worn any markings: by December 1971, it may have received the original insignia of Bangladesh, consisting of a green quadrat with a 'map' of the country in red. The helicopter served as a gunship and was armed with pods for 68mm unguided rockets and a twin 7.62mm machine gun installed in the rear cabin. (Artwork by Luca Canossa)

The sole PAF fighter-bomber unit deployed in East Pakistan in 1971 was No.14 Squadron (crest shown inset), equipped with 16 F-86E Sabres, one Lockheed T-33A and one RT-33A. Most of the Sabres wore a standardised camouflage pattern in RAL 7012 Basaltgrau (basalt grey) and RAL 6014 Oliv (olive) on upper surfaces and sides, and RAL 7001 Silvergrau (silver grey) on undersurfaces, and four were equipped to carry AIM-9B Sidewinder air-to-air missiles, as illustrated here. However, photographs taken at Tezgaon AB after the Pakistani capitulation indicate the presence of a few exceptions painted as illustrated here: in extra dark sea grey (BS381C/640) and dark green (BS381C/641) on upper surfaces and sides, and PRU-blue (BS381C/636) on undersurfaces. Their external armament included SNEB launchers for 68mm unguided rockets installed on centre underwing stations. Also inset is a reconstruction of the sole T-33A captured at Tezgaon, painted in undetermined shades of blue-grey and dark green on upper surfaces and sides, and light grey on undersurfaces. (Artwork by Tom Cooper)

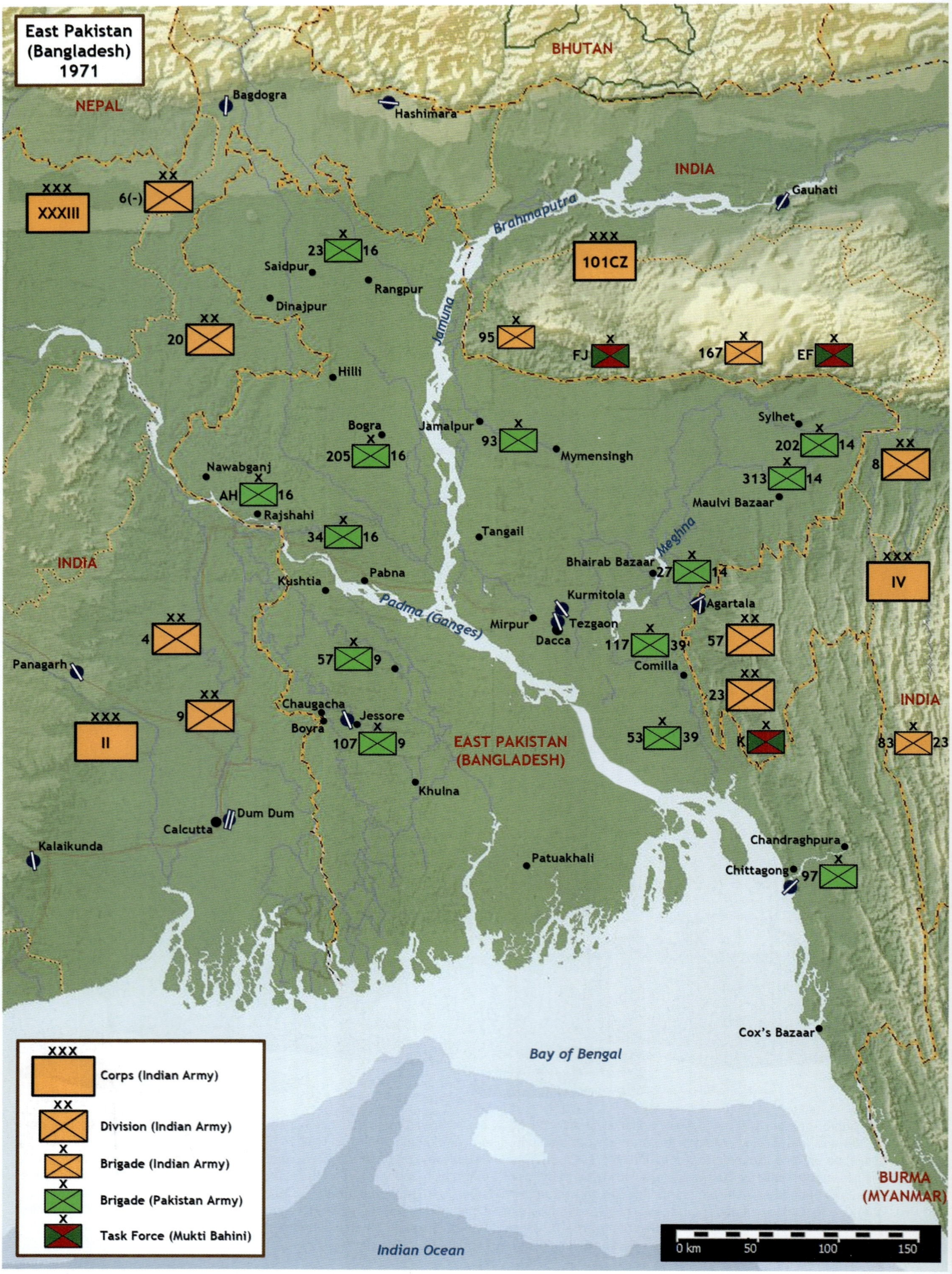
East Pakistan (Bangladesh) 1971
NEPAL
BHUTAN
INDIA
Bagdogra
Hashimara
Gauhati
Brahmaputra
XXXIII
6(-)
101CZ
23
16
Saidpur
Rangpur
Dinajpur
Jamuna
20
95
FJ
167
EF
Hilli
Bogra
205
16
Jamalpur
93
Mymensingh
Sylhet
202
14
313
14
8
Nawabganj
AH
16
Rajshahi
34
16
Maulvi Bazaar
Tangail
Meghna
Bhairab Bazaar
27
14
IV
Kushtia
Pabna
Kurmitola
Agartala
Padma (Ganges)
Mirpur
Tezgaon
Dacca
117
39
57
4
57
9
Comilla
Panagarh
23
9
Chaugacha
Jessore
Boyra
107
9
53
39
K
83
23
II
EAST PAKISTAN (BANGLADESH)
Khulna
Dum Dum
Calcutta
Kalaikunda
Patuakhali
Chandraghpura
Chittagong
97
Cox's Bazaar
Bay of Bengal
BURMA (MYANMAR)
Corps (Indian Army)
Division (Indian Army)
Brigade (Indian Army)
Brigade (Pakistan Army)
Task Force (Mukti Bahini)
Indian Ocean
0 km
50
100
150

Air Strikes and Operation Beaver

With PNS *Ghazi* out of the way, the Indian Navy faced no opposition at sea. The embarked air wing of INS *Vikrant* went into action against targets in East Pakistan on 4 December 1971, when eight Sea Hawks flew their first strike against the port of Cox's Bazar. Later the same day, they also bombed ships in the port of Chittagong. The ship and its air wing saw no action on the next day, but on 6 December, 10 Sea Hawks and two Alizés attacked barges used to move Pakistani Army units in the riverine ports of Mangla, Khulna and Chalna. Three additional attack sorties were flown by Sea Hawks during the afternoon, followed by several nocturnal strikes. After another break, several Pakistani merchant ships and patrol boats were hit by Sea Hawks on 8 December. The deepest strike was flown by Sea Hawks on 9 December, when Lieutenant Commander Kumar Gupta and his pilots were tasked with re-striking the port of Khulna. It was during this attack that the jet piloted by the Indian squadron commander received a heavy hit from the Pakistani air defences, but Kumar Gupta managed to nurse it back for a safe landing on board the *Vikrant*.

The culmination of the Indian Navy's involvement took place on 12 December, when no less than 28 sorties were flown by Sea Hawks – all against the port of Chittagong. This figure implies that some of the involved jets conducted up to three sorties that day. Additionally, the frigates *Beas* and *Brahmaputra* shelled the port of Cox's Bazar and then – along with the destroyer INS *Rajput* and LSTs *Gharial* and *Guldhar* – operated against local merchant traffic.

Out of the blue, and without any preparation, the Indian Navy then decided to make an amphibious landing at Cox's Bazar: the ill-fated Operation Beaver. The *Rajput*, *Brahmaputra* and *Beas* provided gunfire support, while the two LSTs – reinforced by another ship of that kind, INS *Magar* – offered landing support. Since no training, reconnaissance or rehearsal was undertaken, the operation was an abject failure. It is unclear if an anti-mine reconnaissance was conducted, but what is certain is that the LST crews did not even know the depth of the water in which they disembarked their troops, resulting in several drownings. When an infantry company eventually gained the shore, they learned that the Mukti Bahini had already seized the target. Operation Beaver is best veiled behind thick curtains as the second greatest 'snafu' of the naval war; the greatest took place in the Arabian Sea and will be covered in Volume II.

Jagjivan Ram, India's defence minister, visiting INAS 300 during a post-war inspection. Note the 'leaping tiger' insignia of this unit on the nose of the nearest of the Sea Hawk fighter-bombers seen in the background. (Albert Grandolini Collection)

Lieutenant Commander Santosh Kumar Gupta (left), CO of INAS 300 during the war of 1971. Kumar Gupta later rose to the rank of rear admiral, before retiring in 1990. (Albert Grandolini Collection)

A trio of Alizé anti-submarine aircraft warming-up prior to catapult-assisted take-off from INS *Vikrant*. Note the three launch rails for unguided rockets under the wing of each aircraft. (Albert Grandolini Collection)

Demolished warehouses in the port of Cox's Bazar after one of the air strikes by Indian Navy Sea Hawks. (Albert Grandolini Collection)

Air War

If Pakistan had very little to gain – and much to lose – in a full-scale war with India, and if the lack of United Nations interest in East Pakistan's plight showed that as long as Pakistan kept this affair a 'domestic concern' there was a good chance of getting away with it, it might appear strange that when the war officially came, it was a result of a deliberate Pakistani attack on India. However, one should keep in mind that ultimately it was a combination of Indian Prime Minister Indira Gandhi's repeated warnings that time for a peaceful solution was running out and the series of 'border incidents' – actually a gradually intensifying offensive of the Indian Army, supported by the Mukti Bahini, into East Pakistan – that made the implications for Pakistan obvious. If war was inevitable, then it was in its interests to start it at a time and in a manner of its own choice. With lessons of the June 1967 Arab–Israeli War still fresh in everyone's memory, the mass of foreign observers jumped to the conclusion that Pakistan opted to open the official war by launching a drastic, pre-emptive attack on air bases in western India, intending to alter the balance of power. However, recent publications have shown that there was never an attempt to do so. Regardless of what extent it went to run a carefully orchestrated counter-air campaign, the Pakistan Air Force (PAF) eventually produced something far less than a total and sustained effort: seeking to achieve objectives limited in scope and duration, while conserving its own numbers, it deployed far too few aircraft against far too few targets to repeat the Israeli exercise. Unsurprisingly, it achieved very little.[3]

As figures listed in Table 9 show, the balance of power in the air was massively in favour of the Indian Air Force. Arguably, the IAF had to keep a sizeable portion of its fleet in reserve in case of a Chinese intervention, and, just like the rest of the country's armed forces, the balance had to be distributed on two fronts – one in the west and the other in the east. Nevertheless, its total numerical superiority was overwhelming. However, especially after a rather shy performance by the IAF during the 1965 war with Pakistan, the question was whether or not the Indians would deploy their full might. Eventually, as time was to show, the IAF not only survived the opening PAF air strike of the afternoon of 3 December, along with air raids on the following night, but hit back strongly the next morning.[4]

Even then, initial Indian counter-air strikes on Tezgaon AB, the primary PAF base in East Pakistan, can only be described as 'conservative'. Although deploying 177 combat aircraft organised into 13 squadrons (see Table 10 for details) against just one squadron of 16 F-86E Sabres and one T-33A (plus eight helicopters), the IAF did little to knock out the sole PAF radar station or to promptly destroy the ability of the Pakistanis to continue launching combat air patrols. As a result, it lost at least three – and possibly more – fighter-bombers to Pakistani Sabres, and another 10 to ground-based air defences, while downing only three F-86Es. It was only on 6 December, and upon insistence of the CO of No. 28 Squadron, Wing Commander Bhupendra Kumar Bishnoi, that MiG-21FLs of that unit started targeting the runway of Tezgaon with Soviet-made 500kg FAB-500M-62 bombs. In a matter of five extremely precise air strikes, not only this runway, but also that of nearby Kurmitola airport were cratered to such a degree that PAF operations were permanently grounded. For the rest of the war, the IAF enjoyed total aerial dominance over East Pakistan. Not only was it free from aerial opposition while supporting the advance of ground forces, but it was also able to interdict any Pakistani efforts to move reinforcements and supplies along the region's riverine system. Not only were Pakistani F-86Es grounded by air strikes on Tezgaon's sole runway, and eventually captured – mostly intact – after the end of the war, but all the PAF in East Pakistan could do was evacuate its personnel by helicopter to neighbouring Burma.

Table 9: Total Number of Operational Squadrons and Aircraft, IAF and PAF, 1971

Indian Air Force	Pakistan Air Force
8 x MiG-21 squadrons (~160 aircraft)[5]	1 x F-104, 1 x Mirage IIIEP squadrons (12 and 24 aircraft in total)
6 x Su-7 squadrons (~100 aircraft)	3 x MiG-19 squadrons (~60 aircraft)[6]
3 x Canberra squadrons (~60 aircraft)	1 x B-57 squadron (~25 aircraft)
6 x Hunter squadrons (~100 aircraft)	6 x F-86E/F squadrons (~140 aircraft)[7]
8 x Gnat squadrons (~150 aircraft)	
3 x Mystère IVA squadrons (~60 aircraft)	
10 helicopter units	
20 SAM squadrons (6 launchers each)	

Table 10: Indian Air Force, Eastern Air Command, 1971 (units committed to the campaign in East Pakistan)[8]

Aircraft Type	Squadrons & Notes
Hunter F.56 & F.56A	Nos 7, 14, 17 and 37 Squadrons (38 aircraft including 5 two-seaters)
Gnat F.1	Nos 15, 21, 22 and 24 Squadrons (65 aircraft)
MiG-21FL	Nos 4, 28 and 30 Squadrons (54 aircraft)
Su-7BMK	No. 221 Squadron (12 aircraft)
Canberra B(I).56	No. 16 Squadron (8 aircraft, half of the unit)
Total	177 combat aircraft

An F-86E Sabre (serial 1802) of No. 14 Squadron, PAF, after the end of the war. Only four jets of this unit were equipped to carry US-made AIM-9B Sidewinder infra-red homing air-to-air missiles, and the unit found itself fighting against massive odds. Nevertheless, its pilots claimed up to five confirmed kills over Dacca on 4 December 1971, while losing three of their own aircraft. (via Albert Grandolini)

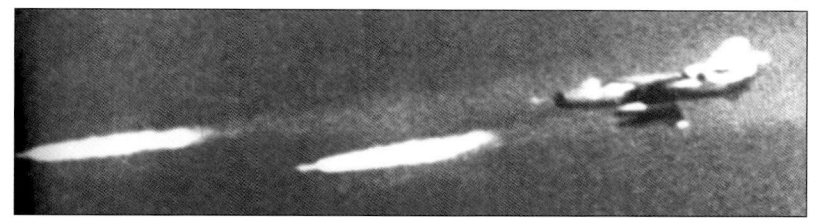

One of the big Su-7BMK fighter-bombers from No. 221 Squadron, IAF, unleashing a pair of 240mm S-24 heavy unguided rockets upon a target in the Dacca area on 4 December 1971. (Albert Grandolini Collection)

A MiG-21FL from No. 28 Squadron, wearing a makeshift camouflage pattern in green and brown, with launch rails for Soviet-made R-3S (ASCC/NATO-codename 'AA-2 Atoll') infra-red homing air-to-air missiles. Visible installed under the centreline of the jet is a single 400-litre drop tank. (Albert Grandolini Collection)

A reconnaissance photograph taken by a Canberra bomber of the IAF, showing a total of 15 craters along the runway of Tezgaon AB – all caused by air strikes by MiG-21FLs of No. 28 'First Supersonics' Squadron, led by Wing Commander Bishnoi. The resulting damage effectively grounded No. 14 Squadron, PAF, for the rest of war. (Albert Grandolini Collection)

Misfortunes of Task Force Alpha

While other dates are also recorded, the Bangladesh Navy came into being on 21 September 1971. Initially, it consisted of two gunboats – the *Padma* and the *Palash* – crewed by 45 men. There were also nine Marine commandos, and, later on, at least four small patrol craft were added.

Tragically, both gunboats were mistakenly hit and destroyed by Indian fighter-bombers on 10 December 1971, during an operation against Mangla seaport south of Khulna along with an Indian gunboat, INS *Panvel*, and vessels of the Indian Border Security Force. The Indian commander of the small Task Force Alpha found no targets at Mangla because a day earlier, Hunters from IAF No. 14 Squadron had attacked and destroyed the base. Undeterred, he decided to proceed north and attack Khulna, and thus moved north of the designated bomb line. Three Gnats from No. 24 Squadron, IAF, located the naval force; two launched rockets at the ships and then returned to use their cannons. Unsatisfied, they turned back for a third attack. The Indian gunboat escaped by manoeuvring and firing at the attacking aircraft, and then beaching itself before the crew abandoned ship. The ships did carry identification panels, but most likely, the Gnat pilots – who were new to this theatre of operations and unfamiliar with Bangladeshi ships – misidentified their targets. Pilots from No. 24 Squadron are known to have claimed the destruction of several boats on that day, and thus they were likely responsible. Understandably, no one wants to talk about 'friendly fire' accidents, no matter how often they happen in nearly every conflict. A Bengali crewman fighting fires on one of the gunboats who refused to abandon ship and was killed, was subsequently awarded his country's highest gallantry award.[9]

Ironically, the Indian naval commander who headed Task Force Alfa was awarded India's second highest gallantry award, the Maha Vir Chakra, for carrying out "most daring and highly successful attacks on the enemy in Mongla and Khulna Ports … Manoeuvring his Squadron through a most hazardous and unfamiliar route, Commander X achieved complete surprise and routed the enemy in Mongla inflicting very heavy losses. Commander X then proceeded to attack Khulna to destroy the enemy entrenched in strength in the port."

Despite the wording of the citation, Mangla had already been destroyed by the IAF. His ignoring the bomb-line led to the deaths of several Bangladesh Navy sailors. He himself escaped due to fancy manoeuvres and firing at the IAF fighters. It was only by sheer luck that he did not bring down any of the Indian aircraft. Major General Jake Jacob wryly has noted the incident, but also said the award was an Eastern Command decision, not just an Indian Navy

The Indian-supported Bangladesh Army included a small naval service –Task Force Alpha. Tragically, that unit's involvement in the campaign proved short-lived, primarily because its overenthusiastic commander ordered it into a position where it should not have been, exposing it to attacks by IAF fighter-bombers on 10 December 1971. This photograph was taken during training in India before the fateful action. (Albert Grandolini Collection)

decision. The last thing the Navy should have done was reward this rash – though undeniably brave – officer with such an award. In his defence, for several months he had been part of a top-secret Operation X, details of which were revealed only 45 years later: he trained several hundred Bangladesh Navy commandos and planned their repeated raids in East Pakistan riverine waters, managing to sink almost 100,000 tons of shipping and severely damaging Pakistan Eastern Command's ability to move between Army positions. Someone had to lead the Bangladeshi sailors and Indian naval commandos. If he operated with the Bangladeshis on clandestine missions, he was well deserving of his Maha Vir Chakra.

Task Force 74[10]

On 8 December 1971, Task Force 74 (TF.74) of the 7th Fleet, United States Navy, was ordered to depart Yankee Station off South Vietnam and deploy into the Indian Ocean. After stopping off Singapore to assemble, the formation – centred on the world's first nuclear-powered aircraft carrier, the giant USS *Enterprise* (CVAN-65) – transited the Straits of Malacca, arriving in the Indian Ocean on 15 December and taking a position west of the Andaman islands. A day later, it reached a point off southern India and Sri Lanka, when it received news that Pakistani forces in East Pakistan had surrendered. With its presence becoming moot, Task Force 74 never entered the Bay of Bengal.

The purpose of this deployment is a topic of frequently fierce discussions to this day – even more so because TF.74's location once it passed Malacca was not publicly revealed for decades after. What did become known was that the Chairman of the Joint Chiefs of Staff of the US armed forces, Admiral Thomas Moorer, and his Chief of Naval Operations, Admiral Elmo Zumwalt, showed no enthusiasm for this mission and considered it pointless. The first scholarly analysis of TF.74's passage was published in 1973, but remained unavailable for many years.[11] While the official Indian history of the 1971 war includes an imaginative account of TF.74 being dispatched to provide cover for a covert convoy consisting of a gunboat, a tugboat and barges spiriting away the Pakistani top brass, the convoy in question was detected while still close to the coast, attacked and forced to beach itself on 11 December, when TF.74 was still assembling off Singapore. Indian Navy officers – politely – remained silent on the matter. USS *Enterprise*'s command history for 1971 and the cruise history were made available but were redacted.

Unsurprisingly, rumours surfaced in abundance. Some have claimed that TF.74 was dispatched to evacuate West Pakistan forces from the East. This is an absurd thesis, considering the ships of the task force lacked the necessary capability. Even once helicopter carrier USS *Tripoli* (LPH-10) offloaded its Marine Battalion Landing Team and retained only 200 troops on board, it could accept only about 1,800 personnel. This might have been enough to collect any Westerners keen to leave East Pakistan, but not the more than 90,000 West Pakistani troops. The Soviet – and modern-day Russian – narrative is that TF.74 entered the Bay of Bengal, trailed by a Soviet naval task force, which then 'surrounded' the Americans and prevented them from an intervention, thus saving the day for India.[12] To call this a work of fantasy would be an understatement![13] As of December 1971, the Soviet Navy had only one destroyer and a supply ship in all of the Indian Ocean. On 5 December, these two ships were replaced by another destroyer and supply ship. All four Soviet vessels were then ordered to stay on station, while replacements – including one cruiser and up to six submarines – were deployed from Vladivostok between 6 and 13 December, but none of the latter reached the Indian Ocean before 18 December, and most only two weeks later. Still, related reports did create a wave of gratitude for the Soviets in India, and in recent years has provoked severe anti-Americanism.

The deployment of TF.74 is also claimed to have prompted Prime Minister Gandhi to authorise the development of nuclear weapons and a break-up of Sri Lanka (to prevent the USN from using Trincomalee as a base against India). However, India had been working on a nuclear weapon since 1969, and waited for its first test until 1974 simply because it had to produce enough fissile material for its first bomb. The US 'intervention' of 1971 was simply not a factor in decision-making about Indian nuclear weapons: on the contrary, it was the first Chinese nuclear bomb test of 1964 that was. Secondly, while there are anecdotes about the Soviets pushing the theme in New Delhi, there is no evidence that the USA actively sought a military base on Sri Lanka – a country about to become politically unstable and descend into a lengthy civil war – in the early 1970s. Indeed, Washington and London had already signed an agreement in the mid-1960s permitting the USA to make use of the island of Diego Garcia in the Indian Ocean.

It was only once a report of the USS *Enterprise* to the US Navy HQ was released in 2015 that the USA finally shed some light onto this affair.[14] It revealed that the Head of the UN relief mission in East Pakistan had indicated that due to the spread and scope of the fighting, evacuation of Western nationals might become necessary. Consequently, USS *Enterprise*, commanded by Rear Admiral Cooper, and escorting warships underway at the Yankee Station were ordered to "proceed immediately" in that direction, and the carrier battle group centred on the USS *Coral Sea* (CVA-41) was ordered to replace them off the coast of South Vietnam. TF.74 reached Malacca on the morning of 10 December and the holding area north-east of Singapore two days later. Over the following two days, a total of 10 ships gathered, and then the entire task force entered the Indian Ocean on 15 December. Underway there, Rear Admiral Cooper's staff planned an operation to evacuate from Dacca about 2,000 civilians by helicopters from USS *Tripoli*: these were to be accommodated in the huge hangar deck of the USS *Enterprise*. However, no order to execute this evacuation ever arrived. In the interim, the British RAF evacuated Western nationals from East Pakistan, eliminating the requirement for a US effort. After only one day of operations at Point Alpha, west of the Andaman Sea, USS *Enterprise* – escorted by guided missile destroyer USS *Decatur* (DDG-319), guided missile frigate USS *King* (DLG-10) and destroyers USS *McKean* (DD-784) and USS *Orleck* (DD-886) – moved to Point Charlie, off the southern tip of India, "to await instructions from higher authority". TF.74 thus spent most of its time in the Indian Ocean monitoring both Indian and Pakistani operations and maritime and air traffic, and then the increasing number of Soviet aircraft and vessels approaching the area, while Cooper's staff continued contingency planning. Due to the lack of suitable diversionary airfields nearby (the use of airfields in East Pakistan was never considered), and a limited number of embarked tanker aircraft, the carrier was limited to keeping 12 jets airborne at the same time, and another 12 on quick reaction alert (QRA): these only flew visual reconnaissance. Eventually, the *Enterprise* was ordered to cease operations in the Indian Ocean on 7 January 1972, and return to Naval Station Almeida in the Philippines, which the ship reached five days later.

Therefore, the US never considered this operation a 'military intervention', or even an attempt to meddle in the Indo–Pakistan War of 1971. At no point during this 58-day-long deployment did anyone in TF.74 consider evacuating the Pakistan Army from East Pakistan. Even a possible evacuation of senior officers was out of the question (moreover, only one flag-rank Pakistani officer agreed to be evacuated via Burma; all others did their duty and went into captivity with their troops), and there was no talk about the *Enterprise* fighting its way into the Bay of Bengal, whether against the Indian or Soviet Navy. TF.74 was not there to fight anyone.

USS *Enterprise* (CVAN-65) – the world's first nuclear-powered aircraft carrier and biggest warship as of 1971 – was the centrepiece of the US Navy's Task Force 74, deployed to the Indian Ocean (though not 'into the Bay of Bengal', as frequently claimed in India) in reaction to the outbreak of the Indo–Pakistan War. Taken during the same year, this aerial view of the 341-metre-long *Enterprise* shows most of its air wing of more than 90 combat aircraft and helicopters on the deck. (US Navy)

CHAPTER 6
WESTERN FRONT, INDIAN ARMY'S II CORPS

Because both Indian and Pakistan Eastern Commands destroyed their records (India after the war and Pakistan toward the end of it), an accurate account of operations is difficult to reconstruct. In India's case, the decision seems to have been motivated by a wish to hide the extent of its involvement in East Pakistan, as it was in breach of international law. In Pakistan's case, it was a standard measure by a defeated force. Whatever the reasons, only a broad overview is possible, the results of which might still be viewed as highly surprising.

Especially difficult is assembling an accurate picture of where Pakistani battalions were at a particular point. For example, the Pakistanis say their 9th Division was fighting with just four battalions by about 6 or 7 December, whereas the detailed ORBAT provided by Pakistani historian Major Agha H. Amin lists eight-and-a-half battalions.[1] An additional problem is Pakistan's proliferation of division and brigade HQs to give the appearance of greater strength than existed. Officially, Pakistan had five divisions and 15 brigades; actually, there were just three divisions and 10 brigades along the 1,700km border. To inflate their strength, Pakistan mixed in paramilitary troops. A battalion might, for example, have only two regular companies; the rest would be Border Rangers or Scouts, and armed police. With three classes of troops intermingled at battalion level, this could not have been good for cohesion. However, as a deception measure, this effort failed: the Indians, thanks to the rebels, had the best possible intelligence.

It was only in recent years that New Delhi came to admit that the ground war in East Pakistan began on the night of 21/22 November 1971, and not on 3 or 4 December. Even that, however, is incorrect, as Indian troops entered Bangladesh for reconnaissance and to help the rebels as early as April 1971, and by October several Indian formations were engaged in combat with Pakistani forces.[2] There was thus no 'lightning campaign' of high-speed manoeuvre that collapsed the Pakistani defences in less than two weeks, as frequently claimed. The battle that took place after 3 December was joined after many weeks of scouting, probing and even all-out assaults by the Indian Army, which subsequently enabled its junior ranks to avoid any approach routes expected by the Pakistanis. It is almost certain that, thanks to the activities of the insurgency, they knew which routes to avoid, and thus emerged from unexpected directions.

II Corps vs 9th Division

The first conventional units of the Indian Army to enter East Pakistan belonged to II Corps. This was a new formation (officially established only on 31 October 1971), commanded by Lieutenant General Tapishwar Narain Raina (who, as a brigadier, had successfully commanded the 114th Brigade at the Battle of Chushul in the 1962 conflict with China). While lacking most of its support services, it still had two complete divisions: the 4th Mountain (7th, 41st and 62nd Brigades) and 9th Infantry (32nd, 42nd and 350th Brigades). To bolster the striking power of Raina's corps, and enable him to keep some units in reserve, the GHQ assigned him the 50th Parachute Brigade from strategic reserve. In total, he thus had 20 infantry battalions, eight artillery regiments, two engineer regiments and two tank squadrons under his command (II Corps would later receive a three-battalion formation designated the Bengal Area Task Force).

The Pakistani Army unit facing II Corps was the 9th Infantry Division, touted as Pakistan's best. It was certainly one of the two best divisions, but by October 1971 it was not in control of all its own brigades, being left with only the 57th and 107th Brigade. Commanded by Major General Shaukat Riaz, the 9th Infantry Division was thus vastly outnumbered, having only eight infantry battalions to face 20 Indian battalions.[3] Its third brigade-sized formation, the 314th Brigade, was an ad-hoc assembly comprising the 5th Wing of the (civilian) police, which included the usual Razakars – all but useless in the conventional battle that was to follow. Even more problematic was the fact that the 9th Infantry Division was supposed to screen no less than 600km of the border with India: each of its eight infantry battalions was thus expected to hold a front line of about 75km. While this sounds like a recipe for a disaster, the Pakistanis were not as badly off as it might appear because of the local terrain, while the Jhenida and Jessore fortresses they manned were strongly prepared and easy to defend. Moreover, the 9th Division had ample stores of ammunition and could hold out for at least a month – had its commander decided to do so.

Niazi's assumption was that the Indian forces would advance towards Jehinda and Jessore with a division against each, and thus have no reserves left to exploit any breakthroughs.

Final Preparations

Raina assembled the elements of II Corps to attack along four axes, which were defended by Pakistan Army units listed (from north to south) in Table 11. The II Corps HQ planned to advance to the Madhumati River during the first phase of operations: the 4th Division was to move north and send a blocking force to the Hardinge Bridge, while the 9th Division would send a similar force to Khulna. These two formations would thus provide flank protection. During the second phase, the corps was to advance to the Padma River. Meanwhile, Task Force Bengal Area – consisting of 1/3rd Gurkhas, 11th Bihar, 12th Garwal and Border Security Force troops – was to advance on Khulna from the south, to provide a diversion and force the Pakistani 314th Brigade deployed there to dissipate its strength. However, while it is known that the 1/3rd Gurkhas advanced east to Satkhira, about a quarter of the way from the Indian border to Khulna, that unit and the 11th Bihar were subsequently withdrawn and sent to Calcutta to embark on an abortive amphibious landing at Cox's Bazar (the previously mentioned Operation Beaver, which was undertaken without planning or reconnaissance). Unsurprisingly, it remains unclear if most of the Bengal Area Task Force was ever committed to the battle.[4]

Riazh's 9th Infantry Division had no option but to conduct a purely defensive operation; his aim was to delay the Indians and then fall back on the Madhumati River as the second line of defence. At least 400 metres wide and up to 13 metres deep in December, the Madhumati was expected to hold off the Indians until foreign intervention became effective or the UN ordered a ceasefire. Only in the event of an emergency was Riaz to withdraw to the Padma River and defend the ferry crossings there.

Table 11: II Corps Indian Army and Pakistan Army Units facing it, October–November 1971

India	Town	Pakistan	Importance
7th Brigade/4th Division	Kushtia	57th Brigade	Hardinge rail/road bridge, allowing turn north to block 16th Division's southern flank or south to Dacca
4th Division (-)	Jhendia	57th Brigade	Northern bastion for Jessore, across the Madhumati to seize two ferries on Padma River leading to Dacca
9th Division	Jessore	107th Brigade	Primary town in south-west sector; after being forced out of Jessore the 107th Brigade was to turn south for Khulna
Bengal Area TF (3 bns)	Khulna	314th Brigade	Southern protection for Jessore, river access to Bay of Bengal

Battle of Boyra

There had already been heavy fighting well inside East Pakistan when Raina ordered his troops to occupy several border enclaves in early November. The biggest battle for a bridgehead was at Boyra, which was taken by India forces on 13 November.[5] The Indian official history coyly remarks that the operation was taken to assess Pakistan's reaction: if so, it was a futile exercise, as the salient seized by the 1st Naga remained undiscovered by the Pakistanis until 23 November. The reason was of a practical nature: the morale of the Pakistani troops was so low that patrols went out only once a week. Even then, this Indian intrusion was quickly eliminated by the Pakistanis.

On 20 November, Raina deployed three battalions from two brigades of his 9th Division – the 1st Jammu and Kashmir Rifles, 19th Maratha Light Infantry and the 4th Sikhs, supported by PT-76 amphibious tanks of the 45th Cavalry and Mukti Bahini – to seize the Boyra salient. The Indian official history says Pakistani counterattacks, mounted by an infantry battalion, were defeated. Indeed, on the same day, the 1st Jammu and Kashmir Rifles – with help from the 2nd Sikh Light Infantry – threw back counterattacks by the Pakistani 22nd and 28th Frontier Force. Undaunted, Riaz counterattacked again, with the 6th and 21st Punjab, supported by a weak 3rd Independent Armoured Squadron, equipped with M24 light tanks, and a field artillery regiment. However, his commanders failed to anticipate the heavy volume of fire from the Indian artillery, and the IAF's air support: unsurprisingly, this effort – which went down in history as the Battle of Garibpur – was quickly defeated by the Indians. At that point, the PAF at Tezgaon AB was ordered into action.

On the morning of 22 November, four F-86E Sabres from No. 14 Squadron approached the Garibpur area. While attacking Indian ground troops, they crossed the border several times. Occurring around 0811 hours, the violation of Indian airspace was promptly detected by IAF radar, and four Gnats from No. 22 Squadron based at Dum Dum airport were scrambled to intercept the raiders. However, the Sabres had returned to Tezgaon before the Gnats could reach the combat zone. The same thing happened with the second Pakistani air strike, launched at 1030 hours.

At 1448 hours, Indian radar detected a flight of four Sabres as they climbed to an altitude of 2,001ft (610m) while searching for their targets. Three minutes later, two Gnats and a pair of MiG-21FLs scrambled from Dum Dum. Led by Flight Lieutenant Roy Andrew Massey, the Indian interceptors divided to attack from two sides. The diminutive Gnats remained undetected and caught two Pakistani Sabres as they were climbing from their second strafing run, positioning themselves right in front of Massey and his wingman, Flag Officer S.F. Soarez: both F-86Es were hit by gunfire, and their pilots – Parvaiz Mehdi Qureshi and Khaleel Ahmed – forced to eject. Both were taken prisoner, while the wreckage of their aircraft fell near the village of Bongaon, inside India. Meanwhile, Massey continued his attack, firing at the Sabre flown by Wing Commander Afzal Chaudry. The Pakistani pilot evaded the first burst, but then his jet received a hit in the port wing, forcing him to hurriedly withdraw into Pakistani airspace. Massey and his wingman broke off and returned to Dum Dum, leaving the remaining Pakistani Sabre to return to Tezgaon, where he claimed one of the Gnats as shot down. Taking place in front of thousands of civilians on the ground, this action went down in history as the Battle of Boyra and was a clear-cut defeat for the PAF, which lost two precious F-86Es, for no achievement in return. While both successful Indian pilots were awarded a Vir Chakra, from that point onwards, the Pakistan Air Force ceased providing close air support for Pakistan Army ground troops along the Indian border.

Indian Army PT-76 amphibious tanks carrying infantry while navigating typical East Pakistan terrain, criss-crossed by fields and irrigation canals. (Albert Grandolini Collection)

Although a total of at least four jets from No. 22 Squadron, Indian Air Force, became involved in the Battle of Boyra, it took only two of them to shoot down two F-86E Sabres of No. 14 Squadron, Pakistan Air Force, and thus win a decisive victory in the struggle for control of the skies over East Pakistan. Subsequently, Pakistani Sabres only flew combat air patrols over the Dacca area. (Albert Grandolini Collection)

Wreckage of one of the 3rd Independent Armoured Squadron's M24 light tanks after the Battle of Garibpur. (Albert Grandolini Collection)

Battle of Khulna

The withdrawal from Boyra occasioned considerable condemnation within Pakistan of Riaz's handling of the 9th Division. The most brutal criticism come from Major (retired) A.H. Amin,[6] who called Riaz "an honest person, but a windbag who knew only to pray and refused to leave the safety of his HQ to lead his men". After the Battle of Boyra, the 57th Brigade entrenched itself on the northern part of the line Jessore–Khulna, and 107th Brigade along the southern part. However, contrary to his orders to stage a fighting withdrawal to the Madhumati River, Riaz then dissolved his division even before the Indians made their next move. After just one of his forward defence positions was overrun by the Indian advance, on 3 December, he not only felt bound to shift his HQ from Jessore to a position midway to the Madhumati River, but was alarmed that the Indians might move swiftly around his flank and not leave time for his two brigades to withdraw to Jheinda and Jessore. By doing this, he violated his explicit orders to hold out until his troops took 75 percent casualties.[7]

The 57th Brigade was now to link up with the PA's 16th Division by crossing the Hardinge Bridge, and the 107th Brigade would protect the flank by withdrawing from the Madhumati River to the Padma, and then to Dacca. Once the division was underway, Riaz lost control of events: instead of exploiting the opportunity to withdraw into the fortresses of Jheinda and Jessore, the 107th headed for the river port of Khulna, and spent the rest of the war putting up a solid fight there, preventing the Indians from taking it before the ceasefire. Unsurprisingly, the 107th's withdrawal was severely criticised at home, but as related by Major General Rao Farman Ali Khan, Niazi's political advisor, Niazi himself gave the order to Brigadier Hayat, commander of the 107th Brigade.[8] Niazi wanted the brigade to hold at Khulna, "pending the arrival of the US 7th Fleet", which means that Niazi was violating his own plan.[9]

Of course, the Pakistani 9th Infantry Division's war didn't end with this. Firstly, many of its troops decided to stick it out in Jessore on their own. Although the Indians secured the town on 11 December, and the Pakistani troops were thus surrounded and bypassed by Indian forces, they held the local cantonment and did not surrender until the end of the war. Secondly, to cover his retreat, Brigadier Muhammad Hayat, commander of the 57th Brigade, assembled an ad-hoc task force with one squadron of M24s from the 29th Cavalry and a company of the 18th Punjab. Professionally led by two majors, they took advantage of the ground and, on 10 December, ambushed the 22nd Rajput, led by two troops of PT-76 amphibious tanks from A Squadron of the 45th Light Cavalry, inside Kushtia. The Indians could not manoeuvre off the road because of swamps, and the tanks and the leading Rajput company were destroyed.[10]

Ironically, this happened right after Raina arrived by helicopter to tell his 7th Brigade to stop advancing so cautiously. A situation then developed where one Pakistani ambush forced the 7th Brigade to stop in its tracks, while the GOC II Corps insisted the entire 4th Division (bar one battalion, which was to advance to the Madhumati River) pursue the enemy. Eventually, the commander of the 4th Division collected and redirected his entire division in the same direction, instead of advancing to the Madhumati.

Meanwhile, the Pakistani 57th Brigade safely withdrew over the Hardinge Bridge to reinforce the 16th Division – at which point it vanished into a black hole, never to be seen again. When the 4th Division redeployed to overrun Pakistani positions on the Madhumati and Padma Rivers, it faced only an ad hoc task force drawn from the HQ element of the 9th Division and support troops equal to two weak battalions. Unsurprisingly, these were easily defeated, but the delay meant the Indian 9th Division was late with moving on Dacca.[11]

An OT-64 armoured personnel carrier of the 7th Punjab (9th Division, II Corps, Indian Army), passing a village during the pursuit of the Pakistani 107th Brigade. (Albert Grandolini Collection)

In the meantime, the pursuit of the 107th Brigade was conducted by the 9th Division of Raina's II Corps. The Indian battalions involved were the 7th Punjab (mounted on OT-64 armoured personnel carriers, APCs), 8th Madras, 13th Dogra and 14th Punjab – the latter supported by PT-76 amphibious tanks of C Company/45th Cavalry and B Company/63rd Cavalry, along with IAF Su-7BMK fighter-bombers. The Indian 42nd and 350th Brigades later also joined the pursuit, except for some 9th Division elements that along with the 4th Division's 62nd Brigade were pinning two weak Pakistani battalions against the Madhumati River's west bank. The Indians crossed the Madhumati and chased the Pakistanis all the way to the Padma, aiming for the ferries at Faridpur and Golundo. Brigadier Hayat then stopped any further advance by deploying the 6th Punjab to hold Khulna. As was the norm in water-logged East Pakistan, there was no opportunity for Indian troops to outflank positions; the only road – constructed next to the Jessore–Khulna rail line – was built on an embankment, both sides of which were marshland. The Pakistanis had laid mines in the water, making passage even more dangerous. Eventually, the rearguard action of the 6th Punjab bought the time necessary for the entire 107th Brigade to dig in along a 10km front near Khulna with (from east to west) the 6th Punjab, 12th Punjab and 15th Frontier Force, while Hayat kept the 22nd Frontier Force, most of the 21st Punjab and two M24 tanks left from the Boyra fiasco as reserve. Once again, marshland prevented Indian units from outflanking the position, and several frontal attacks had to be launched. Eventually, on the night of 15/16 December, the 4th Sikhs managed to get behind the 107th Brigade's 15th Frontier Force. The following morning, the 13th Dogra attacked the Pakistani battalion frontally, overrunning two company positions. Keeping his nerve, Hayat counterattacked and recovered the lost ground. The PA's 107th Brigade was thus still stolidly holding its own when Dacca told it to surrender. The Pakistani officers and troops were upset because they felt that the battle for Khulna had just been joined and they could continue holding the line. But when Dacca announced a general surrender, there was no point in them continuing, and some 3,900 troops who had fought courageously against great odds passed into captivity.[12]

Table 12: 9th Infantry Division, Pakistan Army, Battles of Boyra and Khulna, 3 December 1971

Element	Notes
HQ 9th Division	HQ: Jessore; CO Major General M.H. Ansari
• 3rd Independent Armoured Squadron	M24 Chaffee light tanks (only a few left operational after fighting at Boyra)
• 49th Field Regiment	
• 55th Field Regiment	
• 211th (Independent) Mortar Battery	
57th Infantry Brigade	HQ Jhenida; CO Brigadier Mazoor Ahmed
• Squadron of 29th Cavalry	
• 18th Punjab	
• 29th Baluch	
• 50th Punjab	newly established unit
107th Infantry Brigade	HQ Jessore; CO Brigadier Malik Hayat Khan
• 6th Punjab	
• 12th Punjab	
• 15th Frontier Force	
• 21st Punjab	reconnaissance and support[13]
• 22nd Frontier Force	
• 38th Frontier Force	

Battle of Khulna 10-17 December 1971

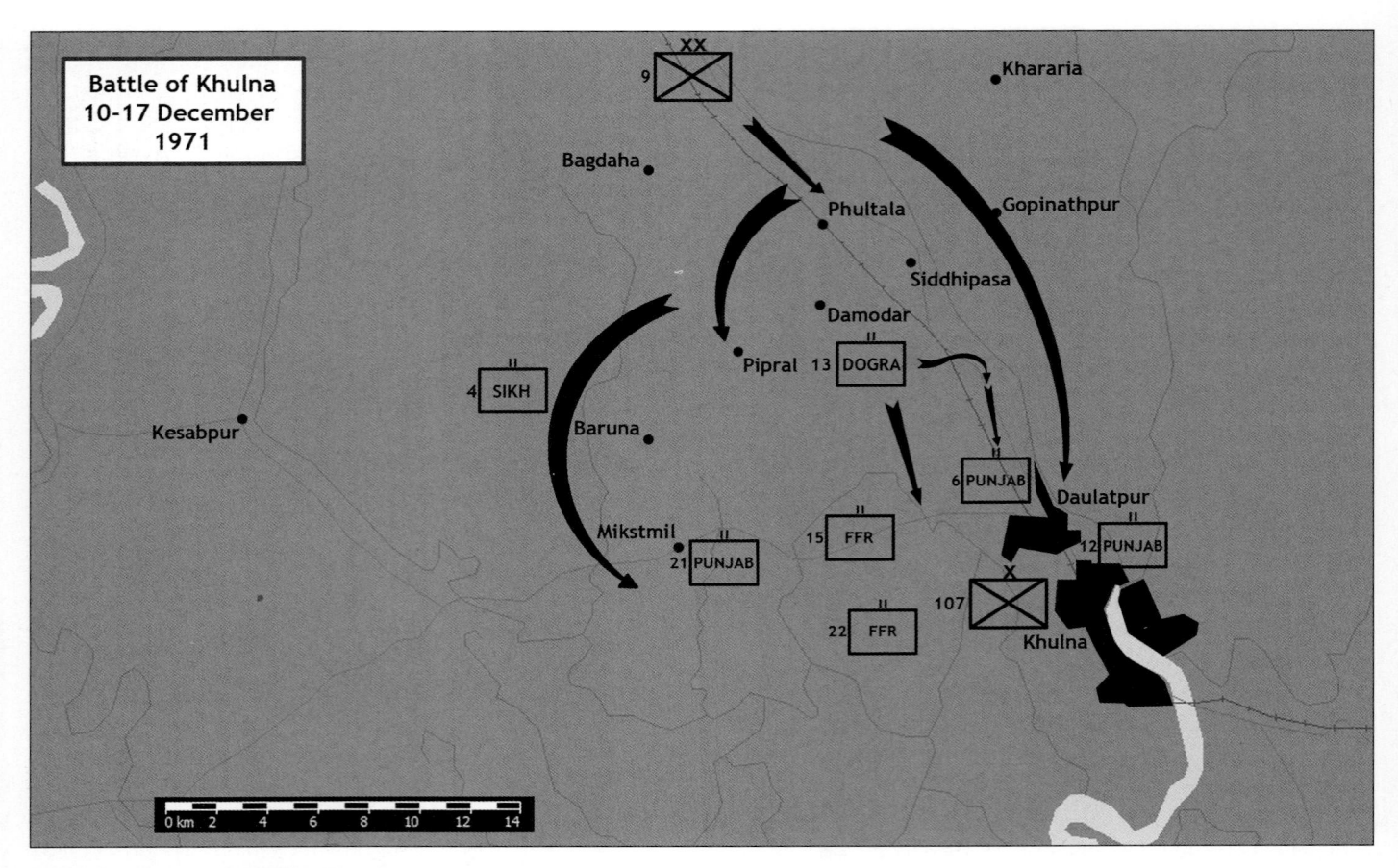

Major General Dalbir Singh, commander of the 9th Infantry Division, Indian Army, taking the surrender of Brigadier Hayat Khan of the 107th Infantry Brigade, Pakistan Army, at the Khulna Circuit House, early on 17 December 1971. (via 1971 Book Series)

One of the M24s of the 3rd Independent Armoured Squadron, PA, which was found abandoned after the war. (Albert Grandolini Collection)

No Sweets for II Corps

Ultimately, while performing its job adequately, the Indian Army's II Corps missed its opportunity to drive on Dacca because of a serious error at multiple command levels. Determining the exact level is difficult, because of an unclear chain of command. Each divisional commander had three superiors: the GOC II Corps, GOC Eastern Command and GOC Army. As mentioned above, the Dacca Plan was developed by the Chief-of-Staff Eastern Command, Major General Jacob, who maintained that Dacca was the political capital, the HQ for Pakistan Eastern Command and the nexus of the region's transport network. All of his superiors felt, however, that taking the capital was an unnecessary risk: Aurora was sure that seizing Khulna in the east and Chittagong in the south-west would lead to the fall of Dacca. Though Jacob was right, and argued his case vigorously, no one signed onto the plan. Had Pakistani forces managed to retreat to Dacca in good order, they could well have held it for two or three weeks until the UN forced a ceasefire on India.

General Jacob – as usual with him, on his own initiative – had arranged for a river flotilla to meet Indian troops at the Hardinge Bridge: ferries were to take two Indian divisions across. The flotilla, named the Inland Water Transport, departed the Calcutta area upon the formal outbreak of war and arrived at Hardinge Bridge on 5 December. There it sat, waiting for orders to embark Indian troops for the run to Dacca. No order ever came; on 18 December, after the war, it went back to Calcutta. Jacob did his best to talk Raina into using the flotilla, but the commander of II Corps, a good, solid infantryman, was trained to first protect his flanks – and did not accept the thesis that speed itself was protecting the flanks – which explains the diversions to Hardinge Bride and Khulna. The GOC point-blank refused, not by saying 'no', but by refusing to debate the matter with Jacob.

After 3 and 4 December, the 4th Division moved swiftly, sending a brigade to capture the Hardinge Bridge and cross the Padma River. The other two brigades successfully attacked the Pakistani 57th Brigade at Jehinda. However, the speedy attack on the bridge failed, and, eventually, the entire division found itself diverting from its primary mission – seizing the ferry crossings on the Padma River – to capture the bridge. By the time the Indians reached this crucial location, the bridge had been blown up, and the 4th Division had to turn around and reposition for an advance to its original objective. This all cost a great amount of time, and it was only on 14 December that the 4th Division managed to force the Padma by using ferries to take two weak battalions to the other side.

A similar situation developed for the 9th Division: while starting the campaign with success at Boyra, subsequently it lost precious time with a diversion towards Khulna and while trying to capture Jessore. After the fall of the latter, it redirected its 32nd Brigade to Khulna instead of focusing on its actual objective: getting to the Padma and capturing one of the ferry crossings there. Eventually, by the time the division reached that river, the war was at an end.[14]

The 107th Brigade of the 9th Infantry Division, Pakistani Army, put up an outstanding fight, successfully distracting most of II Corps into a diversion to Khulna. Had the Eastern Command (and the GHQ in Rawalpindi) not been morally defeated by 10 December, this lone brigade could have enabled the Pakistanis to leave on their own terms, instead of capitulating. Instead, the PA 9th Infantry Division was dismembered, then bypassed by the Indian advance, and then left to abandon Jessore without any real fight: the fortress – and with it one of only three airfields in East Pakistan capable of supporting F-86 jets – fell to the Indians without a shot being fired.

Entrenched Pakistani Army troops in the Jessore sector. (Albert Grandolini Collection)

Truck-mounted infantry of the Indian Army during the advance in the Jessore sector in mid-December 1971. (Albert Grandolini Collection)

Despite the numerical superiority of the Indian armed forces and its allies, the war in East Pakistan in 1971 was no 'Sunday afternoon walk' for the Indian Army. These two of its soldiers were captured in the Jessore area. (Albert Grandolini Collection)

CHAPTER 7
NORTH-WESTERN FRONT, INDIAN ARMY'S XXXIII CORPS

The original areas of responsibility of XXXIII Corps of the Indian Army in early 1971 were Sikkim and West Bhutan. By October of the same year, it was ordered to leave its 17th and 27th Divisions to protect Sikkim, while the 20th Division was redeployed towards East Pakistan. The 23rd Division of IV Corps, usually defending the Siliguri Corridor – where a Chinese offensive could, in theory, reach East Pakistan and thus cut off all eastern India – was to follow in its footsteps. The 20th and 23rd Divisions were followed by the 6th Division, which usually defended Western Bhutan. All three divisions, along with the 71st Independent Mountain Brigade, were reassigned to XXXIII Corps. The corps also received the 340th Independent Mountain Brigade, an armoured task force consisting of one T-55 regiment, one PT-76 regiment and one wheeled infantry battalion, an artillery brigade and an engineer brigade. XXXIII Corps was thereby converted into a potent strike force including six infantry brigades and a small armoured brigade.

All the Pakistani Army had to oppose the powerful XXXIII Corps was its 16th Infantry Division, redeployed to East Pakistan from its bases in the Quetta area, and commanded by Major General Nazir Hussain Shah. This consisted of four brigades (including the 23rd with just one battalion, and the 25th, 34th and 205th, that had to be reinforced by battalions of the Frontier Force), the weakened 29th Cavalry Regiment (operating M24 Chaffee light tanks), the 48th and 80th Field Artillery Regiments and the 117th Independent Heavy Mortar Battery. A crucial part of the 16th Division's positions covered the town of Hilli, which was important as the access point to Bogra, where General Shah's HQ and the HQ of the 205th Brigade were located. The commander of the 205th Brigade, Brigadier Tajammul Hussain Malik, deployed the 32nd Baluch east of the town and the 3rd Baluch to the south, while the 4th FFR – including six companies that consisted of a mix of regulars, Razakars, Mujahids and police – defended the town itself. Each of these formations created platoon-sized and mutually supporting outposts, with numerous pillboxes capable of resisting Indian artillery, connected by an extensive system of communication trenches. Inside Hilli, each outpost was held by a 10-man section of regulars, reinforced by 30–40 Razakars. Fire support was provided by a heavy company operating twelve 106mm recoilless guns, along with 12 light and six medium machine guns. The marshes around Hilli were strewn with mines and barbed wire, which blocked all possible routes bypassing it.[1]

Each Indian brigade dealt with roughly a third of the PA 16th Division, which was deployed from the Siliguri Corridor along the Padma River (its 12th Punjab Regiment is known to have been holding Nawabganj near the Indian border, with a single company at Paksay, north of Hardinge Bridge). XXXIII Corps' commander, Lieutenant General M.L. Thapan, intended his 20th Division to cut the north-western line from Hilli to Gaibanda, isolating two Pakistani brigades, while the 9th and 71st Brigades were to seize

Pakistani Army troops on a truck-mounted patrol in the Rangpur area of the Bogra sector. (Albert Grandolini Collection)

local enclaves and then push south from the Siliguri Corridor. The 340th Mountain Brigade was to take the enclave at Dinajpur, while the 202nd Brigade (of the 20th Mountain Division) was to attack Hilli directly. Finally, two other brigades were to hold the Balurghat bulge north and south of Hilli.

Table 13: XXXIII Corps Indian Army and Pakistan Army units facing it, October–December 1971

India	Sector	Pakistan	Importance
20th Division	North (Siliguri Corridor)	23rd Brigade	CO Brigadier Iqbal Mohammed Shafi; HQ Saidpur or Rangpur; 8th Punjab
9th and 71st Brigades	Centre (Bogra)	205th Brigade	CO Brigadier Tajammul Hussain Malik; 3rd Baluch, 4th FF, 32nd Baluch
	South (Padma River)	34th Brigade	34th Punjab, 48th Punjab, 86th Mujahid, 26th FF
	Rajshahi	25th Brigade	CO Brigadier Mir Ahmed Nayeem; HQ Nator; 32nd Punjab, 13th FF (sent to 205th Brigade), one company from 12th Punjab

The Hilli Problem

The 71st Brigade found a way to bypass the Hilli–Bogra complex and advanced 60km into East Pakistan even before the 'unofficial' start of the war on 21–22 November. Similarly, the 9th Brigade quickly seized most of the terrain east of the Tista River. However, other Indian units failed to match their achievements.

Led by the 8th Guards, the 202nd Brigade attacked Hilli on 22 and 23 November, but the Pakistani 4th Frontier Force Regiment held its position. This was not because the Indian troops were lacking in spirit: the 8th Guards ended the campaign as the highest-decorated battalion (including three Maha Vir Chakras, two Vir Chakras and one Sena medal), and – in recognition of its performance – was given the honour of leading the 1972 Republic Day Parade. It was also not as if the 4th FFR was the best regiment of the Pakistan Army. However, Indian tank shells just bounced off the defenders' pillboxes, and even 500lb (250kg) and 1,000lb (500kg) bombs deployed by IAF Hunters and MiG-21FLs – and plenty of air support was provided – scarcely dented them. The commander of C Company of the 4th FFR, Major Mohammad Akram, probably played a crucial role in the success of the Pakistani defences. For 19 days he appeared everywhere along the line, personally encouraging his men. Tragically, Akram – and Captain Gul Muhammad – were killed as they sought to hold off an assault by either the Indian 63rd Armoured Regiment (T-55s) or 69th Armoured Regiment (PT-76s) with a 40mm rocket launcher (similar to the Soviet-made RPG-7, and probably obtained from China). Akram was posthumously awarded the Nishan-i-Haider (equivalent to the Victoria Cross or Medal of Honor).

Ultimately, the strongpoints of the Pakistani 205th Brigade in the Hilli area gave so much trouble to XXXIII Corps that Thapan decided to deploy his entire 20th Division to destroy the position. However, concerned about Pakistan launching a counterattack into the Pulbari–Barlughat bulge, the 20th Division deployed one of its three brigades on each side of the bulge, and thus attacked Hilli with only the 66th Brigade. For unknown reasons (the reader is reminded that all the related records are missing), the 66th was then reduced to a single battalion, the 6th Guards, making related decisions by Thapan and his staff hard to understand: after all, the Indians were closely informed about the location of Pakistani

A T-55 main battle tank of the 63rd Armoured Regiment (assigned to XXXIII Corps, Indian Army) approaching the Hilli area in late November 1971. (Albert Grandolini Collection)

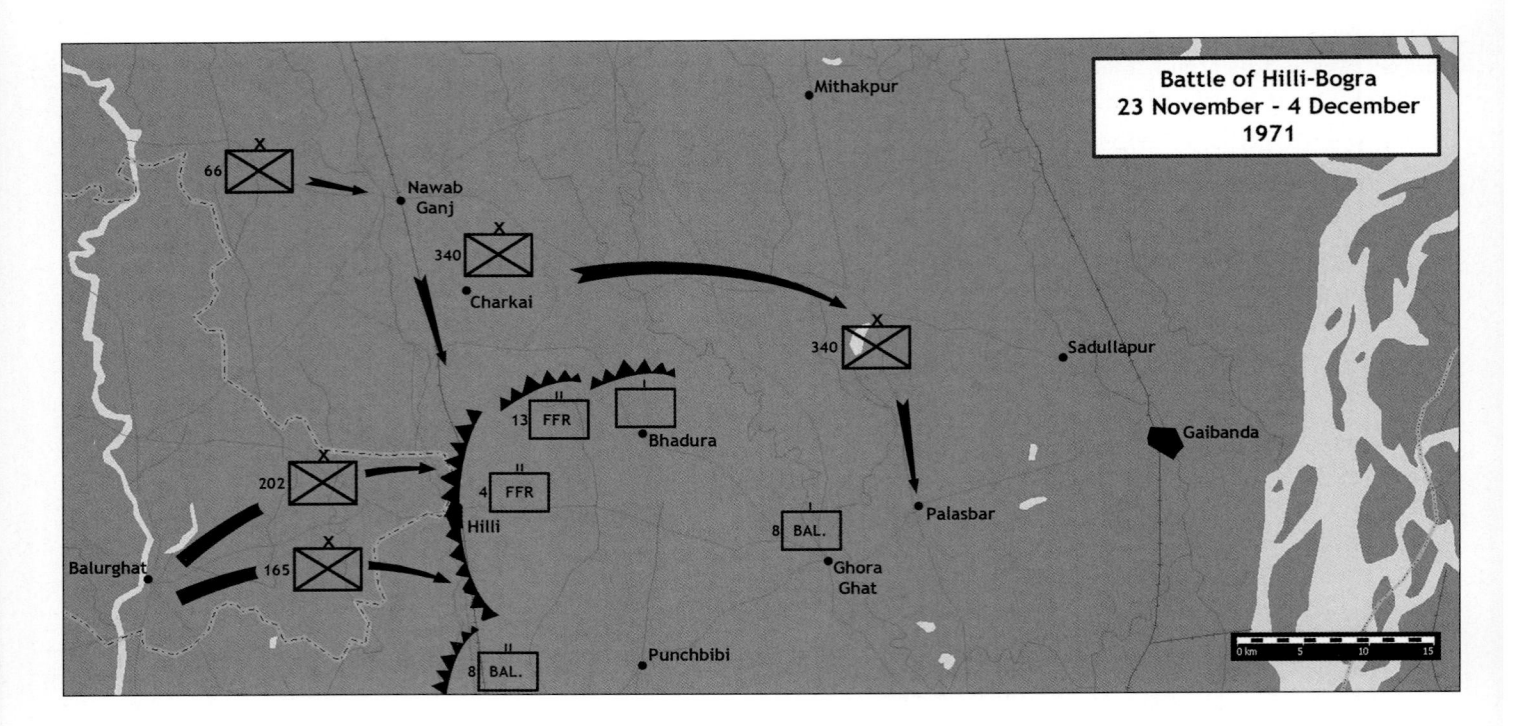

**Battle of Hilli-Bogra
23 November - 4 December
1971**

units, and it is unclear why they expected a four-battalion brigade to weaken its defences by initiating an offensive while facing a division-sized assault. Although a defensive mentality was prevalent in the Indian Army, the operation in East Pakistan was planned as an offensive. Moreover, as well as the 20th Division, XXXIII Corps had the 9th, 71st and 340th Brigades on hand, and should have easily been able to knock out any Pakistani attack while overwhelming the 205th Brigade. Nevertheless, the 66th, 165th and 202nd Brigades of the 20th Division all spent most of the war languishing in their defensive positions, for reasons that remain unexplained to this day.[2]

After almost three weeks of failing to break through at Hilli, despite extensive artillery and air support, on 9 December, the troops of the 6th Guards finally discovered a 'road' – actually a trail through the marshes and across many ravines – to the north of the Pakistani positions, from Chiraj, about 18km from Hilli. This route was protected by only a single platoon because Shah and Malik were convinced it could not support any tanks, never mind a major thrust.[3] However, drawing lessons from their war with China in 1962, during the 1971 campaign Indian forces frequently took trails the Pakistanis thought impassable to outflank their opposition.[4] Eventually, Thapan sent the 340th Brigade to outflank Hilli from the north. By this time, the HQ of the 340th Brigade was stripped of all its battalions, which had been reassigned to other brigades of the 20th Division. However, its enthusiastic commander was quick in seizing the opportunity. He retrieved his battalions and attacked, ending the 'Hilli problem' once and for all on 11 December. After 19 days of continuous Indian attacks, the advance of the 340th Brigade forced Malik and his 4th Frontier Force to retreat towards Bogra. The 340th Brigade promptly exploited the opportunity by turning south for Bogra (with the 202nd Brigade following in its wake a day later). Eventually, they drove through all the way to the Jamuna River, thus splitting the positions of the 16th Division. However, a hastily made plan to ferry the brigade – including its tank squadron and artillery – across the river, so it could protect the 101st Communication Zone's flank as it was advancing on Dacca, was called off.

Even then, the Pakistani garrison at Bogra did not formally surrender until 18 December, and only after repelling successive attacks by the 5th Company, 11th Gurkha Rifles (which collected four Vir Chakras, three Senas, three Mentions in Dispatches and the battle honour of 'Bogra' for its actions).[5] While the defences of the 16th Division thus collapsed during the last week of the war, by the time of the ceasefire of 16 December, its garrisons in Tangpur, Sadipur, Dinajpur, Nator and Rajshahi were all still holding out. The official Indian history quotes Thapan as concluding that there was an "El Alamein mentality", "over centralisation" and a lack of flexible tactics in the north-western front.[6] While probably true this was also the way the Indian Army was trained.[7]

A trio of Indian Army troops in a shallow trench during the fighting for Hilli. The *Naik* (corporal) in the left foreground is armed with a 7.62mm 1A1 rifle (also known as the Ishapore 1A1): this was the Indian version of the British-made L1A1 self-loading rifle, based on the Belgian FN FAL design. The soldier in the background has the Indian version of the Sterling L2A3 sub-machine gun in his hands. Both firearms were standard issue in the Indian Army of 1971. (Albert Grandolini Collection)

A Hunter F.Mk 56 of the Indian Air Force, with two 500lb (250kg) bombs, during a pre-war display. The IAF deployed four units operating this type (Nos 7, 14, 17 and 37 Squadrons) in support of the Indian Army's advance into East Pakistan, and they flew dozens of air strikes against Pakistani positions in the Hilli sector. (Albert Grandolini Collection)

Flamboyant Commander: Brigadier Tajammul Hussain Malik

Brigadier Tajammul Hussain Malik, commander of the 205th Brigade, was a particularly unusual officer. He held a good, politically important position at the GHQ before the war, but volunteered to fight for East Pakistan. He took command of the brigade on 17 November, only five days before the Indian assault began. Even then, he refused to hide like his colleagues, but openly travelled around his sector, inspecting his three battalions while wearing full uniform and flying his flag, exhorting his troops to prayer and to fight to the last. When Indian troops overran Bogra, most of the 205th Brigade surrendered, but Malik refused to do so and ordered the rest of his troops to break out. Trying to escape in a jeep, he was ambushed and captured by the Mukti Bahini. The Bengalis tortured him severely, breaking his arms and skull before delivering him to an Indian Army field hospital. The Indians flew in his captured commander, Major General Nazir Hussain Shah, to order his remaining troops to cease firing. Back in West Pakistan, the brave brigadier was recommended for the Nishan-i-Haider, Pakistan's highest award for courage. This being given only posthumously, he never received it. Nevertheless, Malik was the only brigadier of the Pakistan Army that fought in the East and was subsequently promoted to brigadier general. In 1980, he became involved in a coup attempt against General Zia-ul-Haq, was tried and – after refusing an offer of exile – sentenced to life imprisonment. He was pardoned after Zia's death in 1988.

Portrait of Tajammul Hussain Malik, commander of the 205th Brigade during the war of 1971. (official release)

An amusing incident took place during the 1971 war when the HQ of the 16th Division was ambushed while withdrawing, Shah and his men being forced to abandon their vehicles and seek shelter in the jungle. When the Indians found his jeep, it had a flag plate with two stars on one side, and three stars on the other. This caused much speculation about the Indians almost catching Lieutenant General Niazi himself, who was the only three-star general of the Pakistani armed forces in the East. Little did the Indians know that Niazi had not ventured outside Dacca since the formal start of the war!

The smouldering wreckage of one of several Pakistan Army convoys ambushed during the withdrawal of the 205th Brigade. (Albert Grandolini Collection)

CHAPTER 8
NORTHERN FRONT, INDIAN ARMY'S 101ST COMMUNICATIONS ZONE

Ironically, perhaps the most interesting action of the entire war in East Pakistan in 1971 was the – previously unplanned – advance of Indian troops from Bangladesh's northern border all the way to Dacca. The primary formation of the Indian Army immediately north of East Pakistan at the time was the 101st Communications Zone (CZ), commanded by Major General Gurbax Singh Gill, a HQ with administrative and logistic duties, controlling multiple supply bases for eastern India. Except for two air defence brigades, the only permanently based unit in this area was the 95th Mountain Brigade. Commanded by Brigadier Hardev Singh Kler, the 95th consisted of units trained for operations at altitudes of 1,000–6,000 metres above sea level; unsurprisingly, they not only lacked experience in operating in tropical conditions and flat terrain, but also had less mobility and firepower compared to regular infantry units. Indeed, one of its battalions had just completed conversion to a COIN role and was thus lightly equipped and had no experience whatsoever in conventional operations. Furthermore, the brigade had none of the otherwise omnipresent 106mm recoilless guns and was forced to make do with a handful of 57mm guns per battalion. The rest of its artillery consisted of US-made 75mm howitzers, accurate, but mule-portable and of little use against concrete emplacements. One of its regiments was equipped with Yugoslav-made 76mm artillery, but overall, at the start of the crisis, the entire Eastern Command had just two regiments of medium guns – all old 5.5-in. howitzers from the Second World War.

Ad-hoc vs Ad-hoc

As mentioned earlier, the GHQ of the Indian Army had no plan to advance upon and capture Dacca. Indeed, New Delhi would have been satisfied if enough territory was seized along the border to permit the declaration of Bangladesh as an independent nation. Consequently, the official task of the 95th Mountain Brigade was to control the border between the Brahmaputra and Somshawari Rivers, a front line stretching about 100km as the crow flies (roughly along the line connecting Kamalpur in the west to Duragpur in the east).[1]

Alone the terrain in front of the 95th Mountain Brigade was a major obstacle: a wild country, full of rivers, swamps and streams, with next to no roads. Attempting to move off any of the paths meant vehicles, even tracked ones, soon bogged down. Major General Jacob, Chief-of-Staff Eastern Command, argued that was there was no sign of Chinese activity, and (I believe) he thought he could capture Dacca quickly and then send troops back to the China border. Jacob had his own plans and requested the assignment of four brigades to the 101st CZ. The question was where these would come from? He first tried to get two brigades from the 6th Division in Uttar Pradesh, but this request was refused. He then asked the Army HQ for the release of the 5th and 167th Brigades from the 2nd and 23rd Divisions, respectively, but this too was declined. Finally, he asked for the entire 2nd Division, only to be turned down again.[2] Jacob cannot be faulted for persistence, although it was unclear how four brigades could push all the way to Dacca when transport was simply not available.

However, as mentioned, Jacob had his heart set on Dacca. So he pushed ahead regardless, finding an ally in the 101st CZ's Major General Singh Gill – an aggressive officer who longed to make history but found himself commanding a desk in a backwater, and a no-nonsense soldier who preferred finding solutions to listing reasons why something could not be done. To bolster Singh Gill's assets, Jacob had managed to pry a battalion loose from the 167th Brigade of the 23rd Division at Rangia, in the form of the 6th Bihar. Further reinforcements came with two companies of Indian regulars and perhaps two companies of Mukti Bahinis from FJ Sector, an ad hoc organisation in the 101st CZ which was under the command of yet another keen brigadier, Sant Singh. Thus came into being a plan in which the 95th Mountain Brigade would advance from Kamalpur to Jamalpur and Mymensingh, while the 6th Bihar advanced from Durgapur to Mymensingh. Obviously, such a thrust was a complete improvisation, possible only because local commanders were showing the highest initiative. It comprised a mad dash of 100km, exceeding anything the Indian Army had ever done. The troops were moved using a few army vehicles, but mainly civilian trucks and buses, river boats, bicycles and the ubiquitous taxis of the subcontinent – rikshaws. The 95th Brigade's artillery, for example, was manually loaded on railway flatcars by hundreds of Bengali civilian volunteers and used to provide mobile fire support for the advance. To boost mobile firepower, company commanders were ordered to give up their jeeps, which were jerry-rigged with medium machine guns.

Considering the sorry state of the Pakistani defences in the East, it is unsurprising that the unit facing the 101st Communication Zone was an ad-hoc one, the Pakistan Army 93rd Brigade. Commanded by Brigadier Abdul Qadir Khan, it was one of several formations hastily created in October and November 1971. It had only two regular battalions – the 31st Baluch (Jamalpur) and 33rd Punjab (Mymensingh) – and the 70th and 71st Ranger Wings (deployed in Kishorganj and Bijaipur), with about 550 troops each, along with the 83rd Independent Mortar Battery and a few companies of Razakars.[3]

Battle of Kamalpur

As with so much of Bangladesh, the terrain prohibited tactical bypassing of positions, even while allowing strategic bypassing because Pakistan's force-to-space ratio was so low. Therefore, after initiating its attack on 21 November, the 95th Brigade spent no less than 18 days struggling to destroy and overrun a single company of about 140 Rangers and Razakars – who were protecting Kamalpur with the help of an interlocking network of strongpoints (including concrete bunkers and minefields) –

With anti-tank guided missiles and rocket-propelled grenades still available to the Indians only in relatively small numbers, jeep-mounted 106mm recoilless guns remained the most frequent means of providing direct fire support for infantry. This photograph shows a standard recoilless gun of the Indian Army, a variant of the US-designed M40, manufactured in India by the Ordnance Factory Board under licence. (Albert Grandolini Collection)

before advancing on Jamalpur. The latter was defended by the HQ of the 31st Baluch and – perhaps – two companies. The attack was supported by about 20 close-air-support (CAS) sorties by MiG-21FLs, but most of these had little effect. The Pakistanis held out until the night of 10/11 December, when their commander ordered a breakout. However, the column ran straight into the 1st Battalion of the Maratha Light Infantry, resulting in a pitched battle that lasted four hours. By 0500 hours on 11 December, the commander of the 31st Baluch and about 200 surviving troops broke out. They reached Dacca later the same day, leaving behind 233 dead comrades and 59 wounded. The FJ Sector was then free to reach Mymensingh later that day, and fortunate to face only light opposition. The Baluch captain holding Kamalpur was congratulated for his bravery by the Indian Army chief, General Manekshaw, who ordered special treatment for him after he became a POW. Meanewhile, the commander of the leading Indian Army battalion involved in the attack and his most senior NCO were relieved on the spot.

Tangail Airdrop

By this time, the senior Indian commanders began to get agitated about 95th Brigade's slow advance on Tangail, where a major para-drop was about to take place. Most of them were unaware that the unit had hardly any combat vehicles and was operating on a manpack basis. Unsurprisingly, replenishment took time, as did getting the foot-slogging infantry to Tangail. What was left of the 93rd Pakistani Brigade by this time had managed to slip away.[4]

Because the GHQ in New Delhi anticipated the IAF would quickly establish air superiority over East Pakistan, it decided to deploy the 50th Parachute Brigade for several para-drops. Eventually, nearly all were cancelled because once they did break through, the Indian ground forces advanced faster than anticipated. Thus, the brigade lost the role of establishing blocks behind the Pakistani front lines. One exception was Tangail, a location about 80km from Dacca, which was the HQ of 'Tiger' Siddiqi's powerful group of Mukti Bahini guerrillas.

For this operation, the IAF provided eight Antonov An-12Bs from No. 25 Squadron, 22 Fairchild C-119s from No. 48 Squadron, 27 C-47 Dakotas and DC-3s from Nos 11, 43 and 49 Squadrons, and two de Havilland Canada DHC-4 Caribous from No. 33 Squadron (the latter were used for decoy operations). A few additional An-12s from No. 44 Squadron which were added to the air armada were previously used as bombers (on the Western front), and first had to have their bomb-ejectors removed. Another complication was that the paratroopers were not trained to jump from Dakotas, which required some last-minute remedial training. Loading of the transports took place 'in the open' at Dum Dum Airport, outside Calcutta, in full view of the international press, and the crews of several Soviet An-12s, Canadian Caribous, one American Lockheed C-130 and several C-119s and C-47s involved in delivering relief supplies for Bengali refugees. Sensation-hungry as always, the media was quick to conclude that the 50th Parachute Brigade was involved, and Jacob did nothing to discourage this impression. Moreover, back in New Delhi, the public relations officer of the IAF was told to release photographs of the air drop to the press.[5]

Top cover for the transports was to be provided by MiG-21FLs from No. 4 Squadron and Gnats from No. 15 Squadron.

Eventually, fighter protection proved unnecessary, but none of the senior officers were willing to take any chances. The pilots of supersonic MiG-21s experienced considerable problems when trying to keep in line with the 100km-long stream of transports, because of their minimum airspeed of 450kmph (about 100–150kmph faster than the transports). Consequently, the jets had to zig-zag overhead.[6]

Eventually, the 2nd Parachute Battalion – reinforced by a single battery of the 17th Parachute Field Artillery and commanded by Lieutenant Colonel Kulwant Singh Pannu – landed outside Tangail without a glitch at 1630 hours on 11 December. Undertaken from a height of 1,000–1,200ft (335–366 metres), in a keen, 12-knot breeze, the jump spread the battalion on the ground slightly wider than the planned 2km by 1km drop zone. However, it took the Pakistani Army by surprise and there was no opposition. The battalion regrouped within two hours, met only by jubilant crowds of East Bengalis, many of whom were happy to help collect and carry their equipment. The unit thus quickly secured its main objective, the Poongli Bridge on the Jamuna River, thereby cutting off the 93rd Pakistani Brigade that was withdrawing from the north. During the following night, the paratroopers linked-up with the 1st Maratha Light Infantry, and then ambushed two columns of the Pakistani 83rd Independent Mortar Battery as it attempted to withdraw via the Poongli Bridge. When the Pakistanis realised what was going on, they launched three attacks, but all were repulsed: the paras of the 2nd Battalion latter counted 223 bodies left behind by the enemy. For all practical purposes, that was the end of the 93rd Brigade. Brigadier Qadir surrendered later on 12 December.

A pair of An-12s of the IAF at Dum Dum Airport, outside Calcutta, in the process of loading light howitzers and ammunition of the 17th Parachute Field Artillery. (Albert Grandolini Collection)

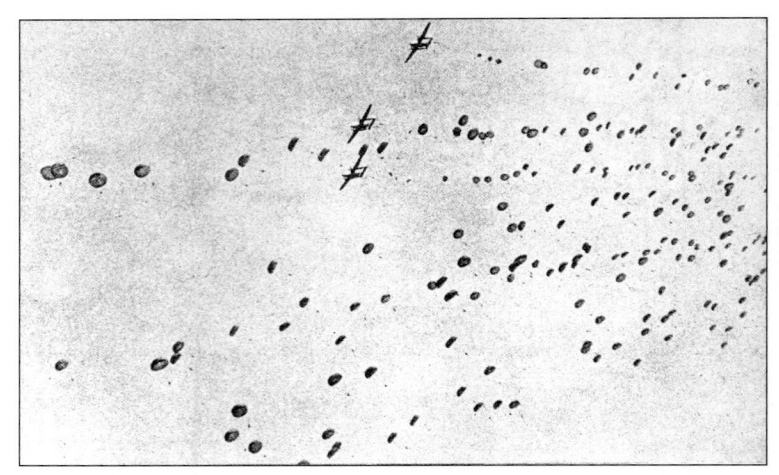

C-119s from No. 48 Squadron, IAF, disgorging paratroopers of the 2nd Parachute Battalion over Tangail on 11 December 1971. (Albert Grandolini Collection)

A pre-war photograph of one of the US-made Fairchild C-119 Packet transports of the IAF (serial IK450). Note the unusual twin-boom configuration of this type. (Albert Grandolini Collection)

Loaded with paratroopers of the 2nd Parachute Battalion Indian Army, and wearing a makeshift disruptive camouflage pattern over the white surfaces on the top of its fuselage, this An-12 (serial BL731/U) rolls down the runway at Dum Dum while underway to Tangail. (Albert Grandolini Collection)

Venerable C-47 Dakotas of Nos 11, 43 and 49 Squadrons, IAF, also became involved in the Tangail airdrop. Visible in this photograph is the example serialled HJ007/D. (Albert Grandolini Collection)

A Hung-up Paratrooper

Understandably, most people reading military history want to read about grand strategy and big operations on which the fate of nations depends. However, it is the myriad of small stories that make a big war. One such story concerns an Indian trooper of the 2nd Battalion Parachute Regiment during the jump over Tangail. The drop involved two C-119s acting as pathfinders, two Caribous dropping dummies at another locality, six An-12s with heavy loads, 20 C-119s and 22 Dakotas. One of the latter was from No. 11 Squadron: as well as the crew of four, it carried two jump instructors and 18 paratroopers. The paras began to jump, but the last man in the stick, an experienced parachutist with 17 jumps, hesitated at the door. Instead of giving the man a few seconds to gather himself, the jump instructors pushed him out, and his parachute started opening while he was inside the cabin. The pilots immediately began to lose control as the aircraft started plunging to earth. The pilots eventually managed to stop the descent 300ft from the ground and get the plane into a climb. One pilot went to the rear door and saw the paratrooper still hung up, with his medium machine gun hitting the tail plane each time he swung in an arc. The Dakota crew executed a series of violent manoeuvres and managed to shake the paratrooper loose, and he landed about 50km outside the drop zone. The Dakota's crew then had to fight the controls of the plane to reach another airfield, flying at only 210kmph, and then land in the dark. The airfield had only six 'goosenecks' (kerosene lamps), which the pilot requested be placed three at each end, and a jeep with headlights stationed at the end of the runway. The pilot, who landed the Dakota safely, recalled: "The port side of the tail plane was badly damaged and most of the stabilizer was missing, the fin had some visual damage, and the rudder surface was completely missing."[1] Luckily for him, the lonesome paratrooper landed in rebel-controlled territory. The insurgents hid him for three days as the Pakistani soldiers searched in vain, and he fought alongside them for several days. He eventually reached the Indian lines in early January 1972. In a big war, so many small incidents of bravery take place that it is impossible to formally acknowledge them all, but this single event highlights the perils that all participants could encounter.

CHAPTER 9
EASTERN FRONT, INDIAN ARMY'S IV CORPS

Commanded by Lieutenant General Sagat Singh, IV Corps of the Indian Army was responsible for the entire eastern side of East Pakistan. Consequently, it was assigned enough units to make it the strongest of the three Indian corps involved in the intervention. From north to south, IV Corps comprised the 8th, 57th and 23rd Divisions, plus several brigade-sized task forces. The first two divisions were organised and trained for counterinsurgency: eight of their regiments had not a single artillery piece, and they were so short on recoilless rifles, mortars and machine guns that superior commanders felt forced to make do by reassigning much of the 8th Division's artillery to the 2nd Division (thereby actually further increasing the risk in the event of a Chinese intervention). Eventually, the HQ of 8th Division – which had the distinction of having spent more years with COIN operations than the entire US Army and the US Marine Corps during the Vietnam War, combined – found itself in control of six brigades, of which three remained with the division, whereas two were kept back for COIN operations. Another brigade, the 61st, was withheld as a reserve. This left only its 59th and 81st Brigades available for an advance into East Pakistan. Unsurprisingly, both had to be reinforced by a total of three battalions of the Bangladesh Army, plus several battalions of the Border Security Force.

Inversely, in terms of ratio of force to length of front, the Pakistani defences were weakest in the east. The PA 14th Division was in the north, with three brigades which had only a total of five battalions between them for a front of over 600km. The 39th Division held the southern part of the Pakistani line, but had only its HQ (i.e., none of the usual division troops like commandos, reconnaissance units and artillery) and four brigades with nine battalions. Facing the 8th Division of the Indian Army were the 202nd and 313th Brigades of the 14th Division, deployed at Sylhet and Maulvi Bazar, respectively. The third brigade, the 27th, was further south at Brahmin Baria, facing the entire 57th Mountain Division of the Indian Army.

Table 14: 14th Division Pakistan Army, November–December 1971

Element	Notes
27th Brigade	CO Brigadier Sadullah Khan; including 12th FF, 33rd Baluch, two troops of M24s, probably one battery of 31st Field Artillery Regiment
202nd Brigade	CO Brigadier Asghar Hussain; including 31st Punjab, companies of Tochi and Thal Scouts, Khyber Rifles, two companies of 12th AK, two companies of 91st Mujahid Battalion, one battery (five guns) of 31st Field Artillery Regiment, 88th Independent Heavy Mortar Battery
313th Brigade	CO Brigadier Iftikar Rana; including 22nd Baluch, 30th FFR, two companies of 91st Mujahid Battalion, one or two companies of Tochi Scouts, one battery of 31st Field Artillery Regiment

boundary with India is counted). To its north it faced Echo Force of the Indian 8th Division, composed of 5th Battalion of the 5th Gurkhas and the entire 1st EBR (the 8th Division had a total of three battalions of the EBR assigned, all from Z Force), and Border Security Force troops. These forces amounted to a brigade's worth of infantry. The Indian 59th Brigade was tasked to pinch-out the Chargram–Karimganj salient to the east of Sylhet; it had already done so before 3 December and was accordingly shifted south to join the 81st Brigade in a drive against the Pakistani 313th Brigade. Meanwhile, to prevent the 202nd Brigade from shifting south, India launched what may have been its first ever airmobile operation, to land the 4th Company of the 5th Gurkhas in several locations south of Sylhet, on 7 December. As of that date, the defences of that city were still intact: the 59th and 81st Brigades of the Indian Army were advancing along two axes either side of the 313th Brigade, and then turned north to hit the southern flank of the 202nd Brigade. Having scattered their opponents, they were soon on the way to Maulvi Bazar and Fenchugani. Hopelessly outnumbered as they were, and subjected to constant air strikes, the Pakistanis were in deep trouble well before the fighting 'officially' began. Nevertheless, they fiercely resisted at each stage,

A grim-faced Pakistan Army officer and four soldiers in the Sylhet sector: they continued offering determined resistance until the bitter end. (Albert Grandolini Collection)

Battle for Sylhet

The 202nd Brigade was responsible for the defence of a 200km-wide front line (and more if the in-and-out nature of the

and it was no easy task for the Indians. Instead of retreating to reach the positions of the 27th Brigade – as ordered – the 313th Brigade broke through and managed to join the garrison in Sylhet. Some attribute this to command confusion, but others say the 313th could not break away from the pursuing Indian troops, and thus turned north instead. Slowed down by stubborn resistance, the 59th and 81st Brigades thus reached the outskirts of Sylhet only on 14 December, after securing huge portions of terrain along the border.

Battles for Akhura and Gangasagar

Holding the southern part of the 14th Division's line – the Akhura sector – was the 27th Brigade of the Pakistan Army. Its responsibility was the defence of the line Akhura–Bhramanbari–Ashuganj–Gharib Bazar. The exact composition of this unit is unclear, and accounts from both sides provide a very different ORBAT. According to Pakistani sources, Akhura was in the middle of the 27th Brigade's 48km-long front line and held by the 12th Battalion Frontier Force Regiment. The northern flank was held by the 33rd Baluch, and the southern flank by the 21st Battalion Azad Kashmir (AK) Regiment, with support provided by 10 field guns, a heavy platoon of the 48th Punjab and four M24 Chaffee light tanks. Ashuganj was on the east bank of the Meghna River, and a major rail/road bridge connected the two towns. What happened at Akhura–Gangasagar is of much interest because it shows how impossibly stretched the Pakistanis were. It Is also an example of a stout defence messed up by a complete failure of the brigade and division commanders.

The Indian Army began investing Akhura in October, and its railway station changed hands several times.[1] However, when the Indian offensive 'officially' began, late on 21 November, no attack took place. Akhura was not hit again until a week later, on 27 November. Having secured this objective, the Indians took several days to mop up the area and bring up reinforcements and supplies before continuing their advance. On 3 December, Gangasagar – some 4km south of Akhura – was secured by the 73rd Brigade of the Indian 57th Division. A single sentence in a book can never describe the ferocity of the fighting for 'some place in the middle of nowhere'. However, Gangasagar was where Lance Corporal Albert Ekka from the 14th Battalion of the Guards Regiment was awarded the sole Param Vir Chakra ('most brave') medal issued to any of the Indian forces during the campaign in East Pakistan. Ekka's company ran into a light machine gun that caused heavy losses, but undeterred, he charged and killed the two-man crew with his bayonet. Although wounded, he insisted on continuing with his company, which then came under fire from a medium machine gun emplaced on the second floor of a building. Ekka charged the building and threw a grenade at the position, killing one enemy soldier and wounding another. The latter continued firing, prompting Ekka to climb over a side wall and enter the bunker to bayonet him. In return, the brave NCO received fatal wounds and died on the spot.

Meanwhile, on 1 December, the 311th Brigade from the 57th Division was working its way around Akhura to the west, while S Force of the Bangladesh Army seized positions to the north of the town.

Table 15: 57th Division Indian Army, November–December 1971

Element	Notes
HQ 57th Division	57th Artillery Brigade (three regiments 75mm, one regiment 120mm mortars), 15th Engineer Regiment
73rd Brigade	14th Guards, 19th Punjab, 19th Rajputana Rifles
311th Brigade	4th Guards, 10th Bihar, 18th Rajput
61st Brigade	Detached to 23rd Division (Comilla); 2nd Jats, 7th Rajputana Rifles, 12th Kumaon

Elements of a Pakistani mortar battery in position in the Akhura sector. Note the heavily protected bunker behind the pit: such fortifications helped the Pakistani regulars to hold out against repeated Indian Army attacks in several places. (Albert Grandolini Collection)

Withdrawal of the 27th Brigade Pakistan Army

While keeping the front company of the 12th Frontier Force Regiment busy with diversionary attacks, the 4th Guards of the 311th Brigade enveloped and then overran a flank position held by a Pakistani platoon and one section. The Guards immediately rushed into the breach, but in the general confusion of battle the headquarters of one of their companies lost contact with its platoons and a lieutenant was sent to find them. He came across one section fleeing to the rear but managed to get them back in their trenches.

This clash exemplified the state of much of the Pakistani Army in eastern East Pakistan at this time, with platoon-sized outposts overrun because they lacked fire-support and had nothing with which to counterattack. The outposts could not support each other because their brigades were spread over much too long a front line, and even if they would have had any reserves, the Indians had so many battalions and so much firepower that they would have swamped any attempts to counterattack. None of this is to denigrate the Indians' superb use of bypassing operations to unhinge – repeatedly – Pakistani defences, but now the race began.

Unable to take the intense Indian shelling any more, the Pakistani troops 'bolted', fleeing the battlefield en masse. A lieutenant colonel from the HQ staff of the PA 14th Division managed to collect a small force of clerks, batmen, military police and two M24s, and counterattacked the 4th Guards in the flank, halting the Indian attack for a moment, but the 27th Brigade could not hold any longer. It had sustained much too heavy casualties in continuous battles since October. On 3 December, the brigade withdrew across the bridge over the Titas River. Lacking explosives and time, the Pakistanis could not blow it up: the Indians quickly seized the bridge and continued their attack, allowing their opponents no opportunity to establish a new defensive line. The 27th Brigade thus withdrew another 14km, to Brahaminbaria, which had previously been developed into a strongpoint with 15 days of ammunition and supplies.[2]

This time, the Indians failed to pursue immediately, so a new defensive line came into being. However, lacking resources to do otherwise, the Pakistanis merely passively waited for the next attack. As usual, the Indians did not take the expected route, but infiltrated the town in small groups, causing a collapse of the defences from within and prompting another withdrawal, this time to the east bank of the Meghna River. At this point, and convinced the Indians had heli-deployed their forces to leap forward, the commander of the 14th Division decided to blow up the bridge without waiting for the mass of his troops to cross from the east bank. The 27th Brigade survived despite the decisions of its divisional commander, managing to get across the Meghna in rivercraft and proceeding into new defensive positions, where – "being presided over" by its brigade and division commanders – it quietly sat out the rest of the war.[3]

In addition to the damage caused by the Bengali insurgency, the Pakistan Army blew up a number of large and small bridges during its retreat, in some cases failing to do so either for the lack of time or of explosives. The engineers here are preparing a demolition of one of the minor bridges. (Albert Grandolini Collection)

Improvised Crossing of the Meghna River

Indeed, the 27th did not move even when the Indian IV Corps did stage a heliborne crossing of the Meghna, 15km to the south, on 9 December. Before the outbreak of the war, Lieutenant General Sagat Singh of IV Corps had complained to Major General Sukhwant Singh (Deputy Director Operations, Indian Army) that he had been given a pointless task of advancing south to take Comilla and Chittagong – as ordered by Manekshaw. Sukhwant Singh hinted in response that he saw no reason why IV Corps should not advance on Dacca. Obviously, this was in defiance of the overall plan, but there it is doubtful that Major General Jacob complained when Sagat Singh showed himself undeterred by the stubborn rearguard action of the 27th Brigade Pakistan Army. Thus, the commander of IV Corps felt free to order the 73rd and 311th Brigades of the 57th Division to cross the fast-flowing, 1.5km-wide Meghna River, "by any means necessary". This might have appeared a routine exercise for any German or US general of the Second World War used to fast-moving operations, but for an Indian Army general of 1971, to disobey orders and improvise to such an extent was unknown. Sagat Singh improvised in fantastic fashion. His most amazing achievement was to get all available Mil Mi-4 helicopters centralised under his command. How exactly he managed that remains unknown, because the helicopters were in urgent demand by all other corps commands. Moreover, Sagath Singh managed to get the 5th Independent Armoured Squadron (with 14 PT-76 amphibious tanks), and then round up every available river vessel his troops could find – in cooperation with insurgent leaders and local boat owners. Thus, on 9 December, the two brigades got across the Meghna. Their subsequent advance was made easier by the fact that the commanders of the 14th Pakistani Division decided that since the Indians were now attacking outside their area of responsibility, there was no need for them to do anything in response.

Studying this campaign, it is easy to see what happened to the Pakistani Army in Eastern Pakistan: each time its units were forced to retreat, they became more demoralised. In short, they had reached their breaking point – and that while in the knowledge their top command was discussing a ceasefire, and with the probable knowledge that no external help was coming. It should not be for us, who were not there, to blandly state that the Pakistani troops should have done better in a land that was alien to them and where they were not wanted.

THE INDO-PAKISTAN WAR OF 1971 VOLUME 1

Table 16: Indian and Pakistan Army Aviation in the East Bengal Campaign, 1971[4]

Indian Army	Pakistan Army
52 helicopters and six fixed wing units	13 helicopters and six aircraft
10th, 11th, 16th Flights (nine SE.316Bs)	Pakistan Air Force (four SE.316Bs)
105th, 110th, 111th Helicopter Units (20 Mi-4s)	No. 4 Squadron, PA (four SE.316Bs)
112th, 115th Helicopter Units (21 SE.316Bs)	No. 4 Squadron, PA (four Mi-8s)
Aviation Research Centre (two Mi-4s supporting SFF)	1 Hiller UH-12E4, PA
Indian Army, six HAL Krishak AOPs	four DHC-2s and two DHC-6s

No Sweets in Comilla

It is likely to appear ironic that even once the units of the 101st Communications Zone and IV Corps had achieved their breakthrough, the mass of the Pakistan Army in East Pakistan was actually still intact. Perhaps the best example was the 39th Division in the Comilla sector: while another of the ad-hoc formations, it consisted of four brigades (with eight infantry battalions), one field artillery regiment, a squadron of M24 tanks, one commando battalion and two Ranger wings. Like the other Pakistani divisions deployed in the province, the 39th had no reserves whatsoever. This became painfully obvious when the 23rd Division of the Indian Army – troops of which had been widely probing for several weeks – discovered several gaps and began shifting its attacks there. As shown in Tables 17 and 18, the 23rd Division had a total of 17 infantry battalions, plus Mukti Bahinis – a strength equal to two full divisions – while the 39th was unable to spare even a platoon, let alone a company or battalion, to reinforce any of its positions. Unsurprisingly, the Pakistani line began collapsing. Nevertheless, nobody surrendered until the ceasefire was called. Indeed, the commander of the 39th Division's 117th Brigade – a former hockey Olympic gold medallist – refused an order from Niazi to withdraw to Dacca, reasoning that surrendering his positions would enable the Indians to drive a wedge between 14th and 39th Divisions, while leaving the Indians a free run to the provincial capital.

While approaching the eastern bank of the Meghna River, the 5th Independent Armoured Squadron (commanded by Major Shamsher Metha) captured three intact PT-76 amphibious tanks of the Pakistan Army during a short clash at Akhaura. All three were promptly pressed into service, thus bolstering the 5th Squadron's strength. (Albert Grandolini Collection)

One of the IAF's Mi-4 helicopters involved in the crossing of the Meghna River. Three squadrons – Nos 105, 110 and 111 Helicopter Units – deployed about 20 helicopters of this type in support of the operation. (Albert Grandolini Collection)

Once Lieutenant General Sagath Singh deployed the infantry of the 73rd and 311th Brigades by helicopters and civilian boats across the Meghna, a pontoon bridge was also constructed by engineers of IV Corps. Light trucks of the 57th Division are shown crossing the latter. (Albert Grandolini Collection)

Table 17: Composition of the 39th Division, Pakistan Army, 1971

Brigade	Sector	Commander	Units
53rd	Feni	Brigadier M.A. Niazi	15th & 39th Baloch, 23rd Punjab, 21st AK
117th	Comilla	Brigadier M.H. Atif	30th Punjab, 25th FFR, two companies from 12th AK, one squadron M24s
91st (Ad hoc)	Chittagong	Brigadier Taskin-ud-din	24th FFR
97th	Chittagong	Brigadier M.K. Malik	48th Baluch, 2nd Commando, 60th & 61st Ranger Wings

Table 18: Composition of the 23rd Division, Indian Army, 1971[5]

HQ 23rd Division	three mountain artillery regiments, one heavy mortar regiment, one engineer regiment, one armoured squadron
83rd Brigade	2nd Jat, 7th Rajputana Rifles, 12th Kumaon
181st Brigade	14th Guards, 19th Punjab, 19th Rajputana Rifles
301st Brigade	4th Guards, 10th Bihar, 18th Rajput
SFF	three battalions of mountain infantry
Kilo Force	31st Jat, 32nd Mahar, 4th & 10th East Bengal, and six companies Mukti Bahini

55

Flamboyant Tibetans: the Special Frontier Force

The Special Frontier Force (SFF) is of interest not because it played an important part in the 1971 war, but because of its antecedents. It has been known as '22 Establishment' and 'Vikas Regiment', and to add to the confusion, at least two of its battalions have even more names (for example, 1st Archer and, in the case of the 4th Vikas, Special Group, which is nowadays considered a special forces battalion). The first three battalions were raised with the assistance of the USA's Central Intelligence Agency in the aftermath of the disastrous Sino–Indian War of 1962. The American intelligence operatives recruited Tibetan refugees both for deep-penetration sabotage operations and as 'stay-behind' troops in the event of another war. For decades, next to nothing was known about the SFF as the Indian Government kept it in utmost secrecy.

The force came to the media's attention in 1974 when several corruption scandals were discovered. Only then did it become known that in peacetime, the SFF's role was reconnaissance along the border with Tibet. Perhaps unsurprisingly, it became involved in several 'unauthorised' operations, part of a dirty little (and private) war in the course of which the SFF troops would venture into Tibet to kill troops of the Chinese People's Liberation Army (PLA). A few were captured, and it is known that the Chinese sometimes beheaded them, while other captives were castrated. The SFF favoured retaliation in the same manner. Since 1975, the unit has been strictly forbidden from operating within 10km of the frontier with Tibet.

However, because the SFF always was, and remains, a tough and well-trained unit, it has been used for everything but official war with China. For example, it led the clearing of the Golden Temple insurgents in 1984 and fought at the Siachin Glacier in 1986 and during the Kargil War of 1999. The Indian Army referred to the SFF as 'Vikas Force', the word Vikas ironically meaning 'development'. In 1971, there were about six battalions of the SFF; there may be 10 today.

It was natural to use the SFF in the 1971 war, and they were assigned their own sector to clear the Chittagong Hill Tracts in the extreme south-east of Bangladesh. While next to no details of its activity have ever been published, it is certain they had almost no vehicles or heavy weapons. New Delhi had to request permission of the Dalai Lama to deploy the unit, which means that (at least up to 1971) it owed its allegiance to His Holiness, and not to the President of India. Ever since then, the SFF's operators share the same pay and benefits as all other regular troops of the Indian Army.

At least as interesting as the force is the man who raised and commanded it for several years: Major General S.S. Uban, a Sikh officer commissioned during the Second World War. He was posted to the British–Indian 22nd Mountain Regiment, an artillery unit with the appellation 22 Establishment. Uban also fought with the Long Range Desert Group, an unusual thing for an Indian officer. He was a brigadier during the 1971 war and known for being a Sikh nationalist and an unorthodox operator. If this was not enough, he was also a mystic. Add to that his personal eccentricities – he was regarded warily as an 'unbalanced officer'. The Indian commander for the Eastern theatre wanted Uban to head a mixed task force in the Bangladesh War. He refused, saying that doing so would damage his military reputation. Surprisingly – an indication of the respect Uban had – the theatre commander deferred to him.

Uban's career had a tragic end. In 1974, he objected to money given to a future army chief for the marriage of his daughter: he was slapped with accusations of corruption and fired at lightning speed. Though the civil authorities judged him innocent, the Indian Army would not take him back. Embittered, he found himself attracted to the Sikh nationalist cause. In 1984, the leader of an Indian Government-sponsored terror group, who had turned against the Government and taken up residence in the Golden Temple, called him in and asked him to organise the temple's defences in case the Government sought to flush him out. One can only speculate that his planning assistance helped turn the Army's attack into a fiasco, with heavy losses. Nevertheless, the Indian Army is persistent, and they cleared the rebels out in short order. Uban thereafter lived quietly and died in the 1990s, leaving a question unanswered: was he a double agent whose ultimate loyalty was to the Indian state, or did he pretend to be anti-Indian to infiltrate the rebel networks?

Uban was so dedicated that when sent to train the Mukti Bahini, he cut off his hair to accompany the guerrillas on their penetrations. For a Sikh, cutting their hair is beyond sacrilege. Interestingly, one account places him in East Bengal as early as November 1970, months before the start of the civil war. Whatever the truth, he was certainly a colourful soldier.

In an interview, one of the three SFF Darpons (brigadiers), each of whom led a battalion, explained how the SFF told the Indian Government in 1971 that either it or the Dalai Lama had to give them a direct order, because this was an offensive war and, as such, immoral. The Indian Prime Minister wrote a personal appeal to the Dalai Lama, whose office issued the order. The idea of employing the SFF was Manekshaw's; the Eastern Command's Chief of Staff decided they must have their own independent sector. The SFF's procedures were unique to them, besides which the rank-and-file spoke only Tibetan. General Uban was considered an unorthodox and sometimes difficult person, so an independent sector suited both sides. There are indications that HQ Eastern Command were not keen on taking the SFF but agreed because it permitted withdrawal of two infantry battalions left in Mizo territory for counter-insurgency duty.

The SFF had already taken considerable territory prior to 3 December, the formal start of the war; it seized the Ramgarh–Demagiri salient,[6] and had also made penetrations eastward from three other bases: Marapa, Bornapansuri and Jarulchuri. The SFF were light infantry, with few vehicles, trained to operate in companies. However, they faced little opposition apart from Pakistan's 2nd Commando Battalion (of unknown strength), plus the usual armed militia. It may be assumed the SFF had considerable support from the tribal groups in the Chittagong Hill Tracts, who had not wanted to be merged with Pakistan and had conducted a low-level insurgency since partition in 1947. The tribes were Buddhists, as were the SFF. Undoubtedly, this was a factor in deciding to use the SFF in this region. The SFF seized Rangamati and shifted its forward HQ there. Two helicopters from the Aviation Research Center, another India–CIA outfit, were sent to help. Their main contribution was to protect 23rd Division's Kilo Force flank as the latter advanced on Chittagong, and destroy the bridge at Dozahari, preventing the escape of Pakistani troops to Burma via the old Burma Road. Manekshaw refused to accept that no one was going to escape via this road, which had fallen into disuse after the Second World War. Since he had no shortage of troops, he could spare men for these irrelevant tasks and no harm resulted from this futile venture.[7]

The Pakistanis usually arranged their defences in strongpoints of 40–50 men, manned by mixed regular troops and police and irregular troops. As in other areas, the intermixing was so extreme that one 50-man post overrun by Uban's men had only 10 regulars. Working with the SFF was the 11th Mukti Bahini Command, and for cover the operation was said to be a Mukti Bahini affair. The defenders usually gave up after an hour or so of fighting. Widely outnumbered as they were, with no hope of reinforcements, it would be unreasonable to expect anything else. SFF casualties during the war included 56 KIA and about five times as many wounded. Helicopter evacuation was difficult because of the jungle terrain, so the wounded were shipped for treatment via river.

A soldier of the Gurkha Rifles during an inspection by General (later Field Marshal) Hormusji Framji Jamshedji 'Sam' Manekshaw. (Albert Grandolini Collection)

12th Gurkha Rifles

As a matter of interest, the SFF often identified themselves as members of the 12th Gurkha Rifles, a fictional regiment. After partition in 1947–48, the 2nd, 6th, 7th and 10th Gurkhas went to the British Army, while the 1st, 3rd, 4th, 5th, 8th and 9th stayed with India. Those Gurkhas that did not want to transfer to Britain went to a new Indian 11th Gurkhas. Today, the British have a three-battalion Gurkha Brigade, into which the original regiments were amalgamated.

M38A1 jeep (right) and trucks of the 23rd Division, Indian Army, waiting to advance once the lines of the 39th Pakistani Division in the Comilla sector were breached. (Albert Grandolini Collection)

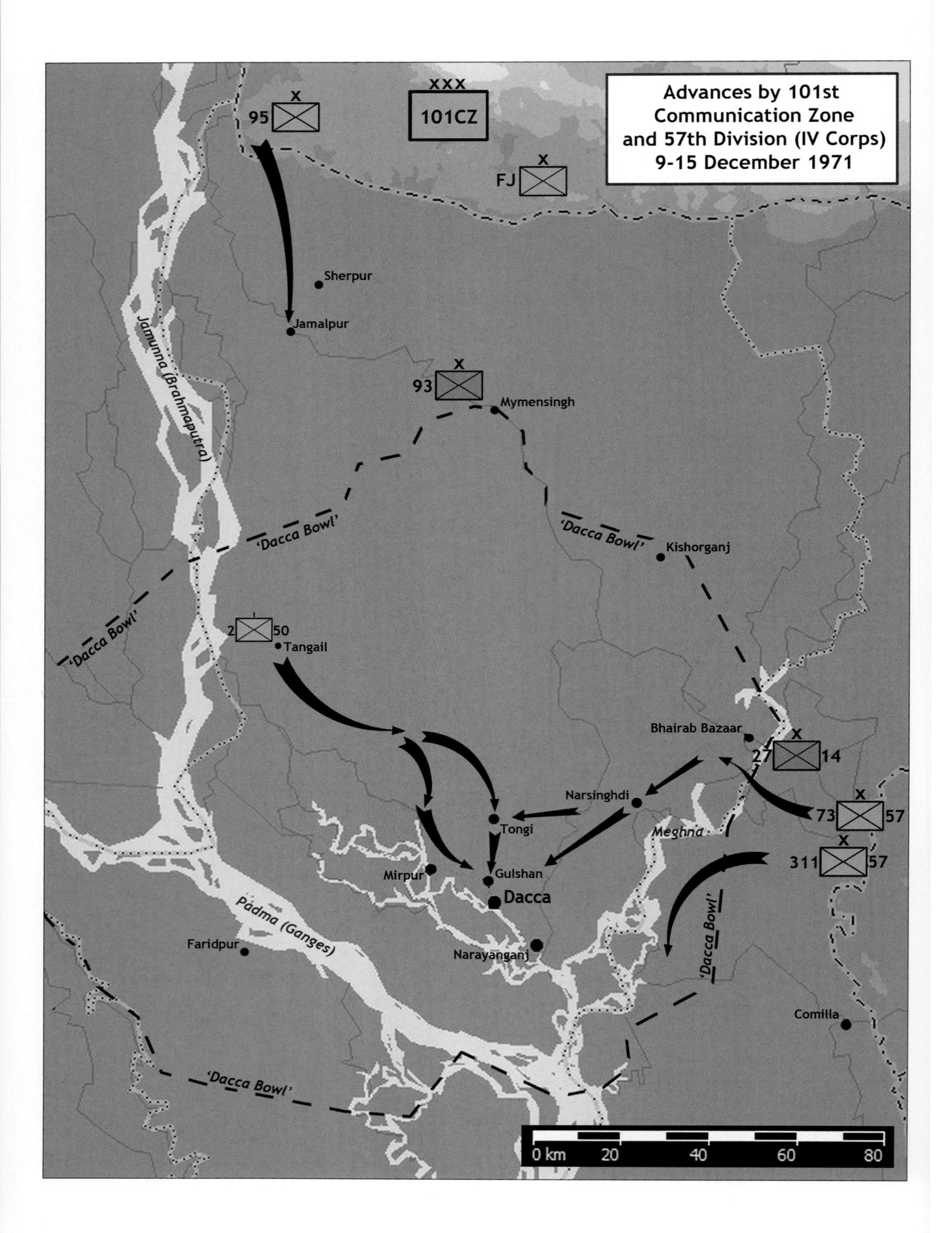

Advances by 101st Communication Zone and 57th Division (IV Corps) 9-15 December 1971

CHAPTER 10
RACE TO DACCA

After crossing the Meghna River on 9 December, and in the true spirit of mobile warfare, the 73rd Brigade, Indian Army, rushed west, reaching an area 70–80km from Dacca by 14 December. Similarly, the 311th Brigade advanced south-west, parallel to the Meghna, arriving 40–50km from Dacca by 15 December. None of this was easy for them because, being mountain brigades, little integral motor transport was available, which meant that these two brigades had to improvise, and like good infantry through the ages, advance by foot. Finally, the 57th Division's third major element – the 61st Brigade, which had been sent to attack Comilla from the north – then turned directly west and, with help of another heliborne operation, crossed the Meghna too. This is how it happened that by 14–15 December, not only the 57th Division, but also the 301st Brigade of the 23rd Division were in a race to reach Dacca: the latter marched from Lakshman (south of Comilla) to Chandpur ferry on the Meghna in just one day. From there it turned north, linked up with the 61st Brigade and then crossed the river.

However, all these efforts were beaten by elements of the 101st Communication Zone, foremost the 2nd Parachute Battalion and 95th Mountain Brigade. After extracting themselves from a joyful reception by the inhabitants of Tangail, Lieutenant Colonel Singh Pannu's 2nd Para and Brigadier Singh Kler's 95th Mountain Brigade moved down the road for Kaliakair. While the 2nd Para was initially left in Tangail, the 95th pressed hard to reach Joydebpur, where it was held up by some resistance on 13 December. A day later, the 2nd Para – reinforced by the Kader Bahini – followed up, marching down the eastern side of the Jamuna River. Singh Pannu and Singh Kler then found a section of newly constructed road, unmarked on the map, which enabled them to bypass the heavily protected Tongi–Dacca road and advance right up to the Mirpur Bridge, at the gates of the capital of East Pakistan. There, they were joined by Major Generals Singh Gill and Gandhary Nagra, who ordered them to push ahead as fast as possible. The 2nd Para thus became the first unit of the Indian Army to enter Dacca, closely followed by the 95th Mountain Brigade. Thus, by 15 December, major elements from six Indian brigades were converging on Dacca.

Major General Gandhary Nagra, commander of the 101st Communication Zone (centre, with the Gurkha hat), briefing troops of the 95th Mountain Brigade, shortly before the war. (Albert Grandolini Collection)

Major General Nagra with one of the Mukti Bahini combatants and Brigadier General Singh Kler, commander of the 95th Mountain Brigade. Nagra and Singh Kler played a crucial role in the final advance on Dacca. (Albert Grandolini Collection)

A convoy of Pakistani Army trucks caught in the open and destroyed by fighter-bombers of the IAF during the last days of the war. (Albert Grandolini Collection)

Non-existing Defences of Dacca

While, with the exception of Jacob, all top Indian commanders were planning the intervention in East Pakistan on the assumption that it would have been pointless to try advancing on such an easy-to-defend objective as Dacca, developments then took their own course.

Nominally at least, Dacca was defended by another ad-hoc formation: the 36th Division. Contrary to other major formations of the Pakistan Army deployed in East Pakistan in 1971, this division had two such massive problems that ultimately it would surrender on contact with the enemy. Firstly, it had no troops of its own: ordered to defend every square metre of East Pakistan, Niazi dispatched its 53rd Brigade to bolster the eastern front against the Indian IV Corps. The division's other major element – the 93rd Brigade – was an ad-hoc formation deployed to defend Mymensingh, and had already been mauled by elements of the 101st CZ. Most of its troops never managed it back to Dacca, and those that did were in pitiful shape, exhausted, hungry and lacking heavy equipment, radios and even boots. Nevertheless, between 14 and 16 December, the Eastern Command Pakistani Armed Forces had managed to collect about 30,000 regular troops, paramilitary troops and Razakars in Dacca. They should have been able to hold out for a while longer, until the UN could effectively intervene in the conflict

However, as with most things military, there is the theory and then there is the reality. The first issue was that the mass of these troops were hopelessly exhausted by an arduous, eight-month-long COIN campaign through the entire monsoon season, followed by 10 days of intensive fighting and then another 10 days of all-out Indian attacks. The units to which they were assigned had already suffered heavy losses, and the morale of their troops decreased with every kilometre of their withdrawal from the border. The monsoon also caused incredible problems: troops from West Pakistan had to endure the kind of rain they had never seen in their life, without proper waterproofing. They were living in waterlogged trenches, in a climate in which everything rots – the human body, leather boots, clothing – and disease is rife. They were also subjected to incessant air strikes and continuous artillery barrages, while lacking their own fire support. Furthermore, their commanders had lied to them – the Indians and the Bengalis had proved their mettle, and there was neither an American nor a Chinese force arriving for their rescue. Finally, the Bengali insurgents, sensing blood, now appeared everywhere, executing any individuals or small groups of Pakistani troops they could find. On top of all of this came the fact that their senior commanders had given up on them. Major General Rao Farman Ali Khan had served as artillery commander for the 14th Division in Dacca from 1967–69, and then as military advisor to the Governor of East Pakistan from 1969–71. As such, he was at the centre of affairs throughout the Bangladesh crisis and has written an insider's account.[1] Quoting from cables between Dacca and the GHQ in Rawalpindi, he made it clear that:

- The civilian governor of East Pakistan, Vice Admiral Syed Mohammad Ahsan, was ready to surrender by 8 December.
- By 9 or 10 December, President Yahya Khan of Pakistan was also set to surrender but wanted the Eastern Command of the Pakistani Armed Forces – i.e., Lieutenant General Niazi – to bear the responsibility.

On 11 December, Farman Ali Khan reached a point at which he flashed an appeal to the United Nations, pleading for its Security Council to arrange for the evacuation of Pakistani troops and civilian officials, in exchange for the establishment of an elected government of Bangladesh. Much bloodshed could have been avoided had the President shouldered the consequences of surrender, as would have been his duty. It is possible that – because the Pakistan Army was still holding its own (except at Jessore) at this time – Yahya could have negotiated an honourable way out for his troops. However, he refused to do so, while Niazi reacted by stressing his superior rank and making it clear that he had not authorised any such approach to the UN.[2]

Final Act

Taking advantage of the split in the Eastern Command of the Pakistani Armed Forces, Manekshaw radio-broadcasted his first request for the enemy commander in Dacca, advising him to surrender. Stressing the humanitarian aspect and guaranteeing observance of the Geneva Convention regarding treatment of prisoners of war, this appeal was repeated twice more. Simultaneously, the Indians launched an intensive propaganda campaign. Moreover, early on 14 December, Indian intelligence received information that the Governor of Dacca, Abdul Motalib Malik, was about to meet the top brass of the Pakistan Army's Eastern Command in the Circuit House in Dacca, at around 1100 hours. The Indians quickly decided to mount an aerial raid on them. Once again, the task was assigned to Wing Commander Bishnoi from No. 28 Squadron, who – only moments before taking off – was briefed that the meeting was taking place at the Governor's House instead. Using tourist maps of Dacca, the four pilots flew their mission each armed with two UB-16-57 pods and 16 S-5K 57mm rockets, which delivered a particularly precise blow. Many of the 128 rockets they fired not only hit the large ancient palace at 1120 hours, but actually passed through the windows to demolish the dining hall where Malik and the generals were forced to take cover under a large mahogany table. Shaken by this strike, Malik promptly resigned, while – reportedly – Niazi subsequently broke into tears and succumbed to the pressure. His response went through to the US Embassy in New Delhi, offering the surrender of the forces under his command in East Pakistan, conditional on several face-saving measures. Washington reacted with stubbornness: it would accept no surrender by Niazi without the knowledge and permission of President Yahya Khan. Consequently, the Americans rushed to establish contact with Islamabad: attempts to consult Yahya lasted from 2300 hours on 15 December until the following morning, when the Pakistani President surfaced to grant his authorisation.

While the IAF spent the morning of 15 December striking selected targets around the city, several 2nd Parachute Battalion officers accompanied Major General Gandharv Nagra on the way to central Dacca to negotiate a surrender of the Pakistani Eastern Command. Initial negotiations were opened via radio, and then the Indian officers used a car to drive to Niazi's HQ – situated in the Hotel Intercontinental, declared a 'safe haven' by the Indian government – only to find themselves confronted by a tall Pakistani guard who roughly told the newcomers that they could not park

Cheerful Indian Army troops atop of one of a squadron of PT-76 amphibious tanks that entered Dacca on 16 December 1971. (Albert Grandolini Collection)

Indian Army troops controlling a group suspected of including Pakistani Army troops, Mujahids or intelligence operatives. (Albert Grandolini Collection)

where they did, because the spot was reserved for the general in command. Harsh words were exchanged before everything was sorted out, but not before one of the Indian officers was shot through the leg by the Pakistanis because nobody told them that the negotiating party was arriving. It was just another of the absurdities that take place during every war. Nevertheless, Nagra's message was delivered. Because he knew Niazi from the days the latter served as a military advisor to the Indian High Commission in Karachi from 1947–48, Nagra opened with a personal note: "My dear Abdullah, I am here. The game is up. I suggest you give yourself to me and I will look after you." The Pakistani reaction can be best gauged by Major General Rao Farman Ali Khan's poignant commentary: "How Nagra had reached Dacca puzzled everybody, but that adequately revealed the state of Dacca's defences."[3]

By this time, the mood within the Pakistani headquarters around Dacca was frantic. Military targets around the city were under constant pounding by IAF fighter-bombers, but operatives of the Special Intelligence Service – the agency that played a crucial role in the extermination of Bengali politicians, doctors, university professors and students, and police officers – were whisked out on board civilian aircraft. Senior Pakistan Army officers were keen to follow, and some had managed to flee to Burma. Nevertheless, Niazi was still making demands. Determined to prevent any further postponements, on 16 December at around 1300 hours, the Indians sent a helicopter carrying Major General Jacob to Dacca, with the text of the instrument of surrender. Two hours later, Nagra led the 2nd Para and 95th Brigade into the city from the north-west, amid news that Major General Ansari had surrendered whatever was left of the 9th Division. Pakistani resistance now ceased and Niazi gave up. Accompanied by Rear Admiral Mohammad Sharif (commander of Naval Eastern Command) and Air Vice Marshal Patrick D. Callaghan (Eastern Air Force Command), Niazi met General Aurora, who was joined by Air Marshal Dewan (Air Officer Commander-in-Chief, East), Vice Admiral Krishnan (Flag Officer Commander-in-Chief, East), Lieutenant General Sagat Singh (commander of IV Corps) and Group Captain Khondakar (Chief-of-Staff of High Command, Mukti Bahini) at Dacca racecourse, and, at 1631 hours, signed the instrument of surrender.

One of No. 28 Squadron's MiG-21FLs during the attack on the Governor's House on 14 December 1971, firing 57mm S-5K rockets from UB-16-57-pods. (Albert Grandolini Collection)

Brigadier General Singh Kler (left), Major-General Gandhary Nagra and two subordinate officers during what became known in India as the Bangladesh Campaign of 1971. Nagra was the officer who wrote the famous "My dear Abdullah…" message to Niazi on 15 December 1971. (Albert Grandolini Collection)

Lieutenant General Niazi signing the instrument of surrender – the capitulation of Pakistani armed forces in East Pakistan – on 16 December, in the presence of Lieutenant General J.S. Aurora (to Niazi's right), and – standing immediately behind – Vice Admiral Krishnan, Air Marshal Dewan, Lieutenant General Sagat Singh and Major-General J.F.R. Jacob. (Albert Grandolini Collection)

CHAPTER 11
CONCLUSIONS

Together with Niazi, over 93,000 Pakistani troops – including 79,676 regulars and 12,192 paramilitary operatives – surrendered to the Indian and Bangladesh liberation forces, making this the largest surrender since the Second World War. The ball was now definitely in the Indian court, and Prime Minister Gandhi exploited the opportunity to condition the exchange of prisoners of war on Pakistan's recognition of the independence of Bangladesh. That said, India treated all Pakistani prisoners of war in strict accordance with the Geneva Convention of 1925, and, once the Simla Agreement was signed and Islamabad officially recognised the independence of Dacca on 2 July 1972, returned all of them home. Indeed, New Delhi went as far as to pardon nearly 200 Pakistani soldiers sought for war crimes by the Bengalis. In turn, and while returning 13,000 square kilometres (5,019 square miles) of territory seized in West Pakistan, India retained a few strategic areas, including Kargil and small parts of northern Bangladesh. Meanwhile, Indian armed forces rapidly concluded their withdrawal from Bangladesh on 12 March 1972.

Instead of meeting Pakistan Army resistance, Indian troops entering Dacca from 15 December 1971 largely encountered joyous masses of local civilians. This jeep crew of the 2nd Parachute Battalion was overrun by Bengalis proudly displaying the original flag of Bangladesh. Visible on the left of the photograph, this flag included a green circle with a red field in the form of the map of East Pakistan/Bangladesh. (Albert Grandolini Collection)

Regular troops of the Pakistan Army marching into captivity after laying down their weapons. Over 93,000 Pakistanis – including 79,676 regulars and 12,192 paramilitaries – surrendered to the Indian and Bangladesh liberation forces, making the end of the 1971 Indo–Pakistani War the biggest surrender since 1945. (Albert Grandolini Collection)

Butcher's Count

As late as two days before the surrender, on 14 December, operatives of the Special Intelligence Service picked up at least 100 physicians, professors, writers and engineers in Dacca, murdered them and dumped their bodies in a mass grave. Many additional mass graves were subsequently discovered in Bangladesh, yet the exact number murdered by the regular Pakistan Army and paramilitary formations in what the US embassy officials in Dacca and New Delhi called "selective genocide", remains unclear. Sources cite figures between 300,000 and 3,000,000, with between 200,000 and 400,000 Bangladeshi women raped. Bihari representatives claimed up to half a million Biharis were killed by the Bengalis, while independent studies cite about 150,000. More dependable are figures about casualties between the combatants. The Indian armed forces lost between 1,426 and 1,525 killed, and between 3,611 and 4,061 wounded. The Pakistani armed forces could have lost as many as between 8,000 and 10,000 killed, plus an unknown number of wounded. Bangladeshi insurgents suffered up to 30,000 fatalities.[1]

Options?

One of biggest questions surrounding the Indo–Pakistan War of 1971 is: was there a chance of avoiding the war, or finding a compromise without a bloodshed? Even with the benefit of hindsight, the conclusion is that the war was inevitable.

Writing good history is a tremendously difficult task, and the issue of causality is possibly the most difficult of historical tasks. It is unsurprising that so many people will say that Yahya – or Bhutto, or Mujib, or Gandhi, or Nixon, or whomever is their favourite bogeyperson – was responsible for the deadlock that led to war. This makes it easier to write history, because writers of such narratives only have to find evidence that supports their thesis and ignore all the disagreeable factors that threaten to disturb the 'perfect symmetry'. On the contrary, if a historian fails to make some dramatic assertion and then try to prove it, he (or she) is losing an opportunity to write a best-seller, and the consequent fame, promotion and often financial reward. But these assertions run afoul of at least three causal historical fallacies: reductive, absolute priority and responsibility. The reductive fallacy assumes there is just one reason for the Bangladesh war. The absolute priority fallacy assumes there was a first cause for the war. The fallacy of responsibility assumes, in this case, that one individual was responsible for the war.

Certainly, individuals are important in shaping history. In each case, however, the individual is not acting alone. She or he is influenced by many other persons and by multiple factors. Moreover, history is not a series of frozen images: it is a dynamic progression where the interaction between leaders changes the course of history's flow, often in a matter of days, sometimes in a matter of hours. A leader's position in February may be different

Hundreds of Pakistani soldiers and intelligence service operatives were detailed by Indian and Bangladeshi liberation forces in the days following the capitulation. While scenes of this kind – showing overzealous Bengalis openly threatening captives with lynching – were frequent, generally, all the Pakistanis were treated in strict accordance with the Geneva Convention of 1925, and were subsequently returned home. This included at least 200 Pakistani soldiers sought for committing war crimes. (Albert Grandolini Collection)

from that in March, and leaders often lie to each other, and to history, as to the cause of their actions. In the case of the Indo–Pakistan War, both sides took great care to destroy their records, thereby creating lots of free space for their leaders to argue as they like. Unless a historian attempts to understand what lies behind a leader's words, a wrong picture is assembled.

The future Bangladesh began working for independence soon after partition. Mujib Rehman, as a charismatic student leader, was a key player in this. Though after the December 1970 elections he may several times have toyed with the idea of assuming the prime ministership of a joint Pakistan, he knew he was not an all-Pakistan leader, nor did he have much interest in what lay outside Bangladesh. In any case, had he agreed to take the joint prime ministership, his followers would have not permitted it. West Pakistan was a distant foreign land for them. Bhutto would not have been averse to taking the leadership of a united Pakistan, but he had no following in the East: moreover, throughout Pakistan, Mujib's party won twice as many seats as he did. To assure his position, Bhutto allied himself with the Pakistan Army.

However, the crucial issue is that the body actually in control over Pakistan – the top brass of its armed forces – had no intention of accepting a partition, or even democracy. The one person who wanted democracy and at the last moment was prepared to even accept partition was Tikka Khan, the Pakistani general blamed for the civil war. If he was at fault, it was his naivety in believing that the people of his benighted country, who had never had democracy before, could – all of a sudden – run a pluralist state. It is not that the people did not want democracy; they did, but those who controlled the levers of power were absolutely determined not to let anybody else run the nation.[2] The unavoidable conclusion is that the 'establishment' in control over Pakistan in 1970–71 was not ready for any kind of compromise. Had President Yahya Khan told his generals he was willing to grant independence to East Pakistan/Bangladesh, he would have been ousted and the crackdown and civil war would have taken place, one way or another.

The second question is: did the Pakistani Armed Forces have the capability to organise themselves better, and successfully defend East Pakistan?

Pakistan's strategy was:

An organised fighting withdrawal, all the way to 'Fortress Dacca', if required.
A riposte in the west to gain territory, to be used for bargaining with India after a ceasefire.

That this was a bogus strategy can be shown by a mental experiment. Suppose Pakistan seizes several districts in Indian Punjab. A ceasefire is declared, and negotiations begin. Is Pakistan going to trade its gains for East Pakistan or for Kashmir? Obviously, for Kashmir. This poses the question: how could a riposte succeed when India was much stronger than Pakistan? The inevitable conclusion is that there was no strategy for the East, except to depend on Indian goodwill. India, being exceptionally timid in its strategic aims, happily showed goodwill in 1947–48 and 1965 by launching no ground offensive. There was, however, considerable air action, in which No. 14 Squadron, PAF – then equipped with just 12 North American F-86F Sabre interceptors, the lone fighter unit in East Pakistan – badly thrashed the IAF with attacks on its Kalaikunda base, setting fire to eight aircraft and causing most of India's air losses in the East. India's forbearance ended in 1971, and after that East Pakistan had no chance.

India's original strategy for East Pakistan was merely to seize a strip around 20km deep all along the periphery and let the rebels declare an independent Bangladesh. Naturally, India's Prime Minister Indira Gandhi could not admit that, because then India could be accused of aggression. Thus, she said she was acting to resettle the refugees. No one bothered to ask what this resettlement would entail, how the refugees would feed and shelter themselves, and how they would defend themselves against the Pakistan Army and armed Pakistani militia and irregulars. The announced strategy and the escalation of fighting at the border from October onward forced Pakistan Eastern Command to abandon the 'Fortress Dacca' concept and move its formations to the border. The border with India is 4,000km in length, and impossible to defend with three divisions. An absolute minimum of two divisions was required as a mobile reserve to make the border strategy work. And given Pakistan had no fighter aircraft to spare for the East, it needed to follow the North Vietnamese strategy against the US, which included vast amounts of anti-aircraft weapons. Of course – and this could be Mujib's point – Pakistan had no intention of defending the East. And if your government cannot protect against external threats, it loses its legitimacy to rule you.

If India had stopped after its initial penetrations, Bangladesh would still have come into existence. In the initial fighting which started on 21/22 November, however, Indian forces easily broke through the thin crust of Pakistan border defences, making penetrations of more than 20km. In one case, Indian troops advanced 60km before the official start of the war. With no mobile reserves, the Pakistanis could do nothing except fall back.

Showing a flexibility and initiative never seen in the independent Indian Army, the plan was then changed to the seizure of the capital, Dacca. The big numerical superiority undoubtedly bolstered India's confidence. A three-to-one superiority is usually cited as necessary to conduct a successful offensive (it appears that India had a five-to-one superiority in combatants). If the attacker and defender have equal numbers and capability, this means thinning out the front to concentrate a three-to-one superiority in the breakthrough sector. A corollary that is seldom appreciated is that, for rapid results, a superiority of nine-to-one is required at the point of contact. No one is saying that the attacker must focus nine divisions against the defender's one; but nine companies against one will get the needed results, or three companies against a platoon. As India was in the remarkable position of having a five-to-one ground superiority in the entire theatre, this permitted it great flexibility and much room for mistakes. The latter inevitably happen in war. The final conclusion is that, with an 11-to-one fighter superiority and East Pakistan blockaded, the outcome of the conflict was inevitable.

The inescapable reality is that no matter what strategy was adopted by the GHQ in Rawalpindi, India would have won: indeed, the wishes of the establishment in Pakistan were diametrically opposite to the capability of its armed forces. This went so far that the GHQ in Rawalpindi issued contradicting orders to Niazi and then punted responsibility to him, explaining that the theatre commander had to decide the best way to fight the war. While making sense from a military point of view, this only stands if the military plan is coordinated with the political plan – and action – which can only be laid down by the government. In the case of Pakistan in 1971, this was the GHQ in Rawalpindi. Niazi was thus caught in a contradictory position. If he defended the core of East Bengal – the Dacca Bowl – India would seize the periphery and declare Bangladesh independent. His correct intelligence information was that this was India's objective. Without mobile reserves, however, there was no way to hold the border with India with just 30-odd regular battalions unless ground was traded for time. Worse, from Niazi's view, was that once the Indians managed to break through the border defences, the Indian Army (or at least Lieutenant General Jacob) 'flexibly' changed its overall war aim, which then became Dacca. By this time, even maintaining unit cohesion became almost impossible for the Pakistan Army, because India switched from attacking fixed border positions to bypassing them. Many Pakistani units were trapped this way. All that remained to hold Dacca was a medley of different units, badly mauled in their defensive battle and having lost cohesion.

Matters were not helped by Niazi's complete absence from the battlefield once the battle was joined, nor by his fondness for wine and women, or that of his generals for making money rather than attending to their duties.

The next question imposing itself about this war is: why and how could the Indian Army move so rapidly into East Pakistan after 3 December 1971? There are at least four reasons, the essence of which are that the situation surpassed even the most optimistic expectations of its political masters and military commanders:

1. The Indian Army had already broken through border defences and was free to exploit.
2. Pakistan had no mobile reserves; once each Indian brigade broke through, there was nothing between it and Dacca.
3. The East Pakistani Mukti Bahini insurgents fought side-by-side with Indian troops, and locals provided a continual stream of intelligence. It is no exaggeration to say that the Indian Army was in possession of superior intelligence about the situation in the entire province: the fog of war was dissipated. Indeed (and, this point is not emphasised in Indian accounts), Indian communication/signals intelligence (COMINT/SIGINT) was excellent, despite its primitive nature and many failings. An example of the Mukti Bahini's help is the assistance it gave to the Indian 95th Mountain Brigade, the first unit into Dacca. The local Mukti unit had 16,000 fighters and controlled the northern approaches to the city, which allowed the Indian brigade to move rapidly.[3] While it is true that the fighting value of the Mukti Bahani was low, its value in providing intelligence and manpower for India's logistics tail was invaluable. Still, even with rebel help, the battlefield was far from transparent and India had to proceed cautiously most of the time.
4. The Indo–Soviet Treaty of 1971 provided critical assurance that India's nemesis, China, would be prevented from intervening. In this respect, Volume II of this book will show that the treaty was as valuable as a single sheet of toilet paper

The scene of another capitulation by an entire Pakistan Army unit. (Albert Grandolini Collection)

It took days, weeks and then months to mop-up the battlefield after the end of the 1971 Indo–Pakistani War. In Dacca, multiple corners of the city acted as collection points for firearms and other equipment left behind by the capitulating Pakistani troops. (Albert Grandolini Collection)

in a supermarket warehouse. Nonetheless, India believed it had the necessary talisman for protection. Later, when India thought the US would intervene, the Soviets assured the Indians they would hold off the US – though there was not the slightest chance they could.

5. The Indian Army had first-rate logistic support in two forms. One was the seven-to-one superiority in helicopters. Though there were only 52 helicopters to support about 250,000 troops, they allowed India to cross East Pakistan's massive rivers (some of which at the monsoon's peak run 15km wide). One, the Meghna in eastern Bangladesh, was still running 1.3km wide. The other logistic support was the free labour cheerfully supplied by the people. If you have enough people, even if they are carrying loads on their heads, on bicycles or on rickshaws, much material can be moved.

No Story: Hamadur Rehman Commission Report

On 18 December 1971, Zulfikar Ali Bhutto was withdrawn from presenting Pakistan's case before the United Nations Security Council on the East Pakistan crisis, and returned home. Two days later, he was taken to the President's House in Rawalpindi, where he took over two positions from Yahya Khan: one as President of Pakistan and the other as first civilian Chief Martial Law Administrator. In an atmosphere in which Pakistan was completely isolated, shocked, demoralised and angered by its sudden defeat, Bhutto then ordered a commission of inquiry on the war and matters related to it. Twelve copies of the commission's report were made, of which 11 were destroyed under unclear circumstances, while the twelfth disappeared

Indian Air Force officers inspecting the sole PAF T-33A captured intact at Tezgaon AB. The aircraft appears to have worn a disruptive camouflage pattern in mid-grey and dark green on top surfaces and sides. In the background are two of No. 14 Squadron's F-86Es (the example to the right has had its fin, rear fuselage and engine removed): five of these were to form the core of the future Bangladesh Air Force. (Albert Grandolini Collection)

without a trace. The commission held a second investigation once the POWs returned home, creating a much shorter report than the original one. It took 35 years for someone to leak this to the Pakistani press, and to this day, this second report is generally referred to as 'The Supplement'. Led by the Chief Justice of the Pakistan Supreme Court, assisted by military staff that included a lieutenant general of the Pakistan Army and all three heads of services, the Supplement contains 10 sections, most of which gave a searing indictment against Lieutenant General Niazi, recommending his court-martial on no less than 15 counts.[4]

A crater in the runway of Tezgaon AB – caused by an air strike by Wing Commander Bishnoi's No. 28 Squadron – after the Pakistani capitulation. Visible in the background are OT-64 armoured personnel carriers of the Indian Army. (Albert Grandolini Collection)

Actually, Bhutto had no interest in justice: he merely wanted the generals discredited so that they could not challenge his rule. Some of those accused were forced to resign, but no other punishment was imposed. Some of the counts against Niazi were for corruption, starting from his time as a divisional commander in West Pakistan, and including smuggling of betel leaf into East Pakistan; some were for association with female escorts; few were for operational failures, i.e., military affairs. The court, headed by Supreme Court Chief Justice Hamdoor Rehman, did not feel competent enough to make a detailed comment on military matters, despite the involvement of four top-ranking generals. Consequently, Niazi was only indicted for irrelevant deployments.

A most intriguing assertion made by the court was that Niazi should have seen when GHQ's orders became irrelevant, and should have acted to preserve his command, regardless of GHQ's orders – through withdrawing his troops back into Dacca – although Niazi has several times requested permission to do exactly that, and it was GHQ that ordered him not to. The reader is left to wonder whether it is possible to court-martial anybody for refusing to disobey his lawful orders. This is certainly a unique interpretation of military law, no matter in what military service.

What went wrong with Pakistan's Armed Forces?

Most of Eastern Command of the Pakistani armed forces was still intact at the time of the capitulation on 16 December. Unsurprisingly, the command has been criticised, not least by Pakistan, for not putting up a better fight. A Soviet veto in the Security Council of the UN prevented the USA from organising a full condemnation of India for invading East Pakistan, which could have been followed by UN-ordered action against India. By 10 December, the Soviets told India to wrap up the campaign because Moscow could no longer protect India. Luckily for New Delhi, ceasefire negotiations started a day later, which bought India more time to make it to Dacca and force a ceasefire. If, however, Pakistan could have held on another week or two, the course of the war would have been different: likely India would have been forced into a ceasefire well before the surrounding of Dacca which marked the final stage of the conflict. Why could Pakistan not have continued for an extra couple of weeks?

What must be borne in mind is that war is not a mechanical event fought by robots. It is, above all, a psychological affair, where the ideal outcome is to break the enemy's will long before his military strength is broken. Pakistan was already in trouble before the formal declaration of war on 3 December, and it was psychologically defeated by the 10th. Pakistani troops were morally and physically exhausted from the eight-month civil war, from which there was no respite because of relentless Indian pressure, exerted directly and through the rebels. Pakistan Eastern Command was physically isolated and unable to get replacements or supplies. Neither the US nor China, whom the soldiers had been led to believe would come to Pakistan's help, made the slightest move. Because Pakistan found itself defending a 1,700km front with the equivalent of just 10 brigades, not only were there big gaps in the front, but there were no reserves. The strategy required two more full divisions as reserves, not to say full artillery and supporting arms for the three division HQs. This, plus air supremacy, allowed India the luxury to strike where it willed; Pakistan was in no condition for a counter-offensive. Wars cannot be won by remaining entirely on the defence. Finally, there was no guidance from GHQ, or from Eastern Command at Dacca. Field commanders and men were vaguely told to do as they saw best. The Pakistanis never saw their commander anywhere near the front lines. On the contrary, they knew him as preferring the company of female 'entertainers', and most of the rank and file as primarily interested in making money through corruption.

Much was made of the hypothesis that Pakistan could hold India on the major river lines, but there is no such thing as a river so wide it cannot be crossed. The true measure is the availability of troops for a given length of river, and the availability of reserves on the defender's side. Pakistan had no reserves, while India had sufficient numerical strength to attack at several points where Pakistan's already sparse defences were unprotected. Pakistan blew up the few bridges and the many culverts on roads/tracks leading to river crossings. But with the help of rebels and its own limited river-crossing engineering capability, India was always able to assemble enough boats to cross. Sometimes helicopters were used to ferry troops across. Certainly, Pakistan managed to delay Indian crossings at several places. Sometimes India crossed before Pakistani troops had a chance to fall back; often it bypassed positions to disorganise the Pakistani defence.

Because Indian troops had been penetrating East Pakistan since October and had created lodgements when fighting became general by 21/22 November, Indian troops made it to Jessore by 5–6 December. At this point Pakistan was supposed to begin its last-ditch, to-the-last-round defence of Jessore, but events determined otherwise. First, the Indians bypassed defences. There was no reason to attack Jessore head-on and suffer needless casualties. Second, Dacca as the final goal had not yet been formulated. Finally, at one point an Indian II Corps probe was thrown back with heavy casualties, enforcing caution on the Indian 9th Division. After the event, it is easy to play the 'should have, would have, could have' game. But to the ground commander at the time, little is clear, much is muddled. Therefore, not only was there little point to Pakistan holding Jessore to the last, but apparently the Jessore brigade was ordered by Eastern Command HQ to fall back on Khulna, without informing GOC 9th Division, to strengthen the small garrison there in anticipation of American intervention. So Pakistani authorities blamed the brigade commander for dereliction of duty, and Indian history criticised the Indian 9th Division for being too timid!

Pakistan's 57th Brigade also did not fall back behind the Madhumati. Instead, it went north and joined the 16th Division. Whether this was disobedience or acting on orders is not clearly known. In the event, a handful of Pakistani troops refused to evacuate the fortress and continued holding out until the ceasefire. Given these circumstances, it speaks well for the professionalism of Pakistani troops that they held out as long as they did. India was unstinting in its praise for the staunch defence that Pakistan's troops put up when they could, despite overwhelming odds. It should also not be forgotten that the Indian Army, in a striking departure from its usual stodgy tactics, fought a mobile war that in itself disorganised the Pakistani defences.

One matter not clearly explained in otherwise detailed Pakistani accounts is just what exactly led the HQ of 9th Division and 57th and 107th Brigades to act as they did? The best composite picture appears to be as follows:

a) The GOC 9th Division was not temperamentally the kind of 'last man, last round' commander that was required to hold Jhendia and Kushtia. This is not to run him down: while Pakistan had plenty of brigadiers of the 'here I stand and here I hold' temperament, the division commanders were definitely wanting. It is repeatedly said in Pakistani accounts that the involvement of the Army in civil administration ever since Ayub's coup of 1958 broke the discipline of the senior officers. There is no reason to doubt this.

b) The CO of 57th Brigade was labelled 'mild' of temperament. Again, this was not what was required when it was either death or dishonour. He seemed obsessed with the danger of being bypassed by the Indians, so much so that he could not withdraw to 'fortress Jhendia', so kept on retreating to stay ahead of the Indians. It is possible that he was less than inspired when his divisional GOC decided to retreat to the Madhumati River line instead of holding the two fortresses at all costs and took his cue to put survival first.

(c) The CO of 107th Brigade was a tough commander, but he had three problems. First, his troops had been badly battered during the fighting at Boyra, the Indians had already knocked out all but two or three of his tanks and he had no air support after 4 December. Both his counterattacks at Boyra were beaten back by Indian troops, inflicting heavy losses. One reason was that he had very little to counterattack with: had he concentrated his troops, the Indians would have poured through the gaps left. There is a suspicion he may have underrated the Indian troops. Second, his defences were breached by Indian attacks. He did not have as much as a platoon to seal the gaps, let alone the fresh battalion he needed. He was therefore concerned he would be enveloped by the advancing Indians. Third, Niazi told him to make for Khulna and abandon Jessore. His first-rate defensive fight from Jessore to Khulna and at Khulna absolves him of any charges of cowardice.

Lessons Learned

There are few military lessons to be learned from the Indo–Pakistan War of 1971. India had overwhelming military superiority and eight months to prepare and train. With East Pakistan blockaded, and fighting in a hostile country, there was no way Pakistan could have won. Had it adopted a Dacca Bowl strategy, it might have held off India long enough for international intervention. Yet, in the long run, this would have made no difference, because while evacuation of its forces under UN auspices could have been negotiated, an independent Bangladesh would have still come into being.

Nonetheless, there are geostrategic and political lessons aplenty.

The first lesson is that it is very difficult for a relatively small country divided into two wings and faced by a much larger hostile country to defend itself. For such a country, adopting a permanent aggressive posture toward its much bigger neighbour is unproductive. At the end of the first Kashmir War in 1948,

The Pakistani armed forces left behind sizeable stocks of ammunition and supplies: most of these were subsequently used to equip the newly established armed forces of Bangladesh. (Albert Grandolini Collection)

India was willing to accept the status quo which left one-third of Jammu and Kashmir with Pakistan; Pakistan, however, was not. Its single-point domestic and foreign policy agenda became recovery of Indian Kashmir. An outright invasion of Kashmir in 1965 proved abortive. It could hardly have happened differently, given that India had two-and-a-half divisions (many still raising) to every one of Pakistan's, and an air force and navy four to five times bigger than those of Pakistan.

Consider Egypt. It fought Israel four times: 1948, 1956, 1967 and 1973, or one war about every eight years. For the 1973 conflict, Egypt utilised every help its ally the USSR could give. When 1973 ended with only a partial success, did Egypt retire and prepare for a fifth war? It did not. Instead, it allied with Israel's patron/ally the US, receiving billions in military and economic aid, and made peace. Sometimes one must forget one's ideological aspirations and face reality. Pakistan continues refusing to do so to this day. Indeed, it launched two major insurgencies in India: in Punjab from 1982–96, and in Kashmir from 1987. Pakistan believes India will at some point get tired and give up. Is there any evidence of this? None. To the contrary, India has shown it is able to fight multiple insurgencies at the same time for decades until it wins. Today, India has a seven-to-one population advantage and a 10-to-one GDP advantage over Pakistan. Why should India compromise?

The war of 1971 was not of Pakistan's making and the country knew it was in a weak position. Despite past disparities, Pakistan had choices. The simplest was to let East Pakistan go after the elections. Yet politically, this was not possible. But Pakistan still had options. One was to stall until the 35th and 37th Divisions – both in the process of establishment since November 1971 – were ready to be sent to the East, and the 9th and 16th Divisions were filled out. Another possibility was to bring forward the raising of the 35th and 37th Divisions to June, when it became clear India was intervening in East Pakistan. But Pakistan has spent decades saying it did not have the money to do so. An alternative was to adjust political goals. Apparently, Pakistan could not do that. Another alternative was to follow the Chinese advice to shift the model to a people's war. However, Pakistan – proud of its spit-and-polish army that outdid its old masters, the British, in the matter of ritual – could not accept this concept. Finally, Pakistan could have shifted its political goals and made up with India. Obviously, this was out of question. In that case, nothing could help but to continue as it was: fight another war when India ran out if patience and lose it too. In similar fashion, nowadays Pakistan fantastically insists that its nuclear weapons will stop Indian retaliation for its actions in Kashmir.

When Pakistan reinforced East Pakistan from March–May 1971, choosing to increase its force level, it refused to accept that basic tactics and strategy cannot be violated. When strong reserves are lacking, a thin border defence based on the slogan "not a centimetre of our sacred soil" cannot work. Even with strong reserves, forward defences need to give way to absorb the impact of an enemy attack. A brittle, static defence will break; restoring it without reserves becomes difficult. In this regard, it appears that Pakistan failed to study even the German and Soviet experiences in the Second World War. The Red Army would give up as much ground as it needed to, to fully absorb the German offensive. But in the main, when Hitler's generals asked him to let them fall back in the face of enormous Red Army offensives, he refused. For all their vaunted battle skills, the Germans were then forced to take huge losses in men and equipment which they could ill afford and were forced back anyway. Unsurprisingly, modern Pakistan strategy does now permit withdrawals.

But, readers will say, to give up even 10km around the border meant Bangladesh's independence could be declared. That is true, yet this is a problem without any solution because the Pakistanis had put themselves in a strategic situation where they had assured their own defeat.

BIBLIOGRAPHY

Albrecht, G., *Weyers Flotten Taschenbuch 1977/78: Warships of the World* (München: Bernard & Graefe Verlag für Wehrwesen, 1978).
Amin, Major A.H., *Why Military Defeat in 1971: The Qualitative Destruction of Pakistan Army between 1955 and 1971* (Mazen Consultants/Military History Centre, 1999).
Arpi, C., 'The Tibetans who fought the 1971 War', Rediff.com (10 January 2012).
Aurora, Lieutenant General J.S., 'The Fall of Dacca', *The Illustrated Weekly of India* (23 December 1973).
Dupuy, Colonel T.N. and Blanchard, Colonel W., *The Almanac of World Military Power* (2nd Edition) (London: Arthur Barker Ltd, 1972).
Ganapathy, V., 'Battle of Bogra', *Scholar Warrior* (Spring 2013).
Gill, J., *An Atlas of 1971 India–Pakistan War: Creation of Bangladesh* (Washington: National Defense University, 2003).
Hamoodur Rahman Commission Report about 1971 East Pakistan Bangladesh Debacle (nasirlawsite.com).
Hardy, P., *The Muslims of British India* (Cambridge: Cambridge University Press, 1972).
Hiranandani, G.M., *Transition to Guardianship: The Indian Navy, 1991–2000* (New Delhi: Lancer Publishers LLC, 2009).
Jacob, J., *Surrender at Dacca: Birth of a Nation* (New Delhi: Manohar, 1997).
Jagan Mohan, P.V.S. and Chopra, S., *Eagles over Bangladesh: the Indian Air Force in the 1971 Liberation War* (New Delhi: Harper Collins, 2013).

Karrar, Agha, *Witness to Carnage* (Lahore: Paramount Marauder, 2012).
Khan, F., *Pakistan's Crisis in Leadership* (Islamabad: National Book Foundation, 1973).
Krishnan, N., *No Way but Surrender: An Account of the Indo–Pakistan War in the Bay of Bengal, 1971* (New Delhi: Vikas, 1980).
Majumdar, R. and Pusalker, A.D. (eds), *The History and Culture of the Indian People, Volume X* (Bombay: Bhartiya Vidhya Bhawan, 1963).
Mason, F.K., *The Hawker Hunter F.6* (Leatherhead: Profile Publications, No. 4).
Mason, F. K., *The Hawker Hunter Two-Seaters* (Leatherhead: Profile Publications, No. 167)
Niazi, Lieutenant General A.A.K., *The Betrayal of East Pakistan* (Karachi: Oxford University Press, 1998).
Prasad, S.N. (ed.), *Official History of the 1971 India–Pakistan War* (New Delhi: History Division of the Ministry of Defence, 1992).
Querishi, Major General (ret.) H.A., *The 1971 Indo–Pak War: A Soldier's Narrative* (Karachi: Oxford University Press, 2002).
Raghavan, S., *A Global History of the Creation of Bangladesh* (Cambridge: Harvard University Press, 2013).
Raghavan, S., *Fierce Enigmas: A History of the United States in South Asia* (New York: Basic Books, 2018).
Rao Khan, Major-General F.A., *How Pakistan Got Divided* (Karachi: OUP Pakistan, 2017).

Salik, S., *Witness to Surrender* (Karachi: Oxford University Press, 1978).

Salunke, Colonel S.P., *Pakistani PoWs in India* (New Delhi: Vikas Publishing House, 1977).

Sinh, R., *A Talent for War: the Military Biography of Lt Gen Sagat Singh* (New Delhi: United Services Institute of India, 2003).

Sisson, R. and Rose, L., *War and Secession: Pakistan, India and the Creation of Bangladesh* (Berkeley: University of California, 1990).

Stern, J. and Abbas, H., *Pakistan's Drift into Extremism: Allah, The Army, and America's War on Terror* (New York: M.E. Sharpe, 2004).

Sukhwant Singh, *India's Wars since Independence* (New Delhi: Lancer Books, 2009).

Tajammul Hussain Malik, *The Story of My Struggle* (Lahore: Jang Publishers, 1991).

Tufail, Air Commodore K., *Against All Odds: Pakistan Air Force in the 1971 India–Pakistan War* (Warwick: Helion & Co., 2020).

Zaki, Colonel Khalid M., *Through the Lens of Operational Art: 1971 Bangladesh Campaign* (Fort Leavenworth KS: School of Advanced Military Studies, United States Army Command and General Staff College, 2012).

ENDNOTES

Introduction
1. For details on publications in question, see Bibliography.

Chapter 1
1. Majumdar, pp.305–336, & Hardy, pp.232–235. There are many books on the partition of India, and scholars are advised to read a few and find one that makes the most sense to them. Apart from Mujumdar, I find the work by the British author Hardy the most neutral, despite this being accused of 'anti-Muslim bias': actually, he explained the Muslim 'side of the coin' fairly.
2. Jalal, p.248.
3. G.W. Choudhurt, 'The Last Days of United Pakistan'.
4. Querishi, pp.7–24.
5. Arpi.
6. S. Cordera, 'India's response to the 1971 East Pakistan crisis: hidden and open Reasons for Intervention', Journal of Genocide Research (2015), pp.45–62.
7. A study from 2011 (see M. Quencez, 'Floods in Bangladesh and Migration to India, The State of Environmental Migration 2011 Study', available at labos.ulg.ac.be) estimated that 20 million out of 150 million Bangladeshis were at risk of natural disasters. Considering the population in 1971 was 75 million, this means that about 10 million were at risk.

Chapter 2
1. Dupuy et al., pp.317–18.
2. Such calculations sometimes prompt the question whether Yahya Khan's decision to return to democracy, announced in 1970, meant that the Pakistan Army anticipated trouble in East Pakistan? From what is currently known, this seems unlikely. On the contrary, the Pakistan Army considered the Bengalis a "cowardly rabble, easy to get sorted out by a whiff of grapeshot".
3. The original capital of Pakistan was Karachi. In 1960, the construction of a new capital began outside Rawalpindi, where the GHQ of the Pakistan Army was stationed: the result was the city of Islamabad – relatively close to the Indian border, but nestled in the foothills of the Himalayas, and positioned in the heartland of the Army supporters (Pothwaris, Paharis and Hazarawals), and thus easy to defend – became the capital on 14 August 1962.
4. World Bank, 'Comparing India and Pakistan by Economy', 30 August 2019.
5. Moreover, while it appears 'logical' to subtract 10 mountain divisions from India's total and thus conclude that Pakistan and India had a division parity, nothing of that kind was the case. To hold China defensively, India required only five divisions, not 10. Moreover, one Pakistan Army division was in East Pakistan, and the experience from the 1965 war should have shown that not only the 4th Mountain Division, but also the 23rd Division were redeployed from the north to the western front line.
6. With martial law in force all over West and East Pakistan, military officers were performing both the role of civil administration and military commanders. This diminished their effectiveness as soldiers, and morally – and financially – corrupted the generals of the Pakistan Army.
7. Many sources insist on the presence of between 12 and 14 battalions of the Pakistan Army. The best guess is that 12 omits the East Pakistan Regiment battalions, and 14 includes two battalions sent from the West before the crackdown.
8. Although the PAF designated them the 'F-86E', the Sabres in question were actually Canadair-manufactured Sabre F.Mk 6s, with a bigger wing, a more powerful engine and the British-made Martin-Baker ejection seats. All were originally manufactured for the German Luftwaffe and acquired in a famous deal paid for by Iran. As such, they were actually more powerful than the F-86Fs delivered by the USA nearly 10 years earlier.
9. Mandeep Singh Bajwa & Ravi Rikhye, 'East Bengal Regiment of Pakistan Army in 1971', www.orbat.info (2003).
10. While it may seem odd that the 5th, 6th and 7th Battalions were faithful to Pakistan, it is likely that the greater percentage of their soldiers were Punjabi. This was also true of the Frontier Force and Baloch Regiments, and later of the Sind and Northern Light Infantry Regiments raised after the 1971 war. One company each from two of the battalions defected to the Indian Army when they were sent into action in the West.
11. The name is ironical, because Mir was a Bengali revolutionary who fought the tyrannical big landlords, declared independence from British rule, and when the landowners asked the British for help, he fought the British too. His men were armed only with bamboo staves and a few swords and spears. His fort had bamboo walls. After several minor clashes, the British decided to take decisive action in 1831, and sent a force of 100 cavalry, 300 infantry and two guns against him. The fort's bamboo walls proved surprisingly resilient to the artillery, but the outcome was never in doubt given Mir had no firearms. The rebels were defeated and Mir died in the fighting, and was commended by the British officer for his bravery. Titu Mir remains, to this day, one of Bangladesh's greatest heroes. Doubtless the Pakistan Army meant well in naming the exercise after him, but little did they know they would take the British place in a colonial war of suppression, 140 years later. As a point of interest, Titu was also the first Islamic fundamentalist to set up rule in South Asia. He met the founder of Deobandi Islam on his travels, was converted to its hard line, and as well as fighting landlords and the British, was also busy killing Muslims who refused to join his 'crusade'.
12. The USA might have intervened in the case of India making major gains in West Pakistan, but from the first day of the East Pakistan revolt, the US knew that East Pakistan was lost.
13. Readers are advised that all orders of battle are actually 'photographs fixed in time': they kept changing as required by operational conditions.
14. Ever since 1947–48, the Pakistanis have shown a strong predilection for going on the offensive, but also the tendency to fail to think things through and to thus get themselves into serious trouble. It seems that due to the emphasis on aggressiveness – based on the above-mentioned myths about their 'racial superiority' – commanders of their armed forces do not like to spend time preparing and practicing. Although 'Who Dares Wins' is the motto of the British Special Air Service (SAS), it does not imply acting foolishly and recklessly.
15. Rao Farman Ali Khan, pp.149–152.
16. Based on Niazi, *The Betrayal of East Pakistan*.

Chapter 3

1. Karrar, *Witness to Carnage*.
2. Unusually for a rebel commander, Osmani did not promote himself to a higher rank. At the minimum he could have made himself a major general: considering he eventually found himself – at least nominally – in command of around some 80,000–90,000 guerrillas, he would have been justified in assigning himself the rank of lieutenant general. However, not only did he keep his rank from retirement, but his brigade commanders also kept their original ranks as majors.
3. Mukti has multiple meanings in Bengali: 'liberation' is probably the closest English analogy, but it also stands for 'salvation/redemption'. Fauj means 'armed force' and Fauji is a soldier', while Bahini means 'armed force/battalion/cohort'.
4. Jacob, pp.66–67.
5. Based on Gill's Atlas. Officially, New Delhi has provided a different laydown, as follows:
   North-west (XXXIII Corps)
   Central (from the Indian border south to Dacca)
   Eastern (IV Corps)
   South-west (II Corps)
6. Of course, some Pakistani sources stress that the pre-1971 redeployments were undertaken because India was already preparing to invade for some time. This assumes that New Delhi would know that in December 1970 East Pakistan would vote for separation. It is enough to say that there is no evidence in support of such a remarkable degree of prescience.
7. Jacob, *Surrender at Dacca*.
8. Whether India would then ask the new nation to invite it to finish the job is not something I know. I make no excuse for this and other lapses in my research; I came to history past the age of 70, when Professor Walter J. Ladwig III at King's College London generously accepted me as his PhD student. The result was the thesis 'Indian Military Coercion, 1947–2017: 33 Case Studies'. At the time, my work was focused on the military and operational matters and I saw no need to take advantage of my stay in India from 1970–89 to learn about its wars by talking to the principals.
9. I am unclear how Jacob got around the Army chief.
10. The reader is advised not to assume that this is anything like the 'entire story': a great deal of related affairs remain unknown and are going to remain unknown. Perhaps the best example for the volume of the unknown is provided by Major General Sukhwant Singh. As of 1971, he had relinquished command of the 12th Infantry Division in Rajastan, to assume a crucial position: the Deputy Director Military Operations, Indian Army. Before and during the war, the Chief-of-Staff used him to keep an eye on field commanders. In the 30 pages of his account on the planning process for the war (Sukhwant Singh, pp.49–80), he never mentions Major General Jacob. Moreover, he cryptically says that after the war, some officers claimed more credit than was due them to them. In his sole reference to Jacob (p.280), he praises him as a progressive officer, and says when he (Sukhwant) took over the 12th Division, he sought the latter's detailed notes made while Jacob was commanding the division on how to conduct the formation in the event of war. This is an admittedly small piece of evidence that he had no animus against Jacob. In the way of ideas, more than one person can produce the same proposal. It is possible that General Sukhwant came up with the concept independent of General Jacob, who had pushed the idea from the very beginning. Moreover, Sukhwant implies that Dacca was the objective from the start. While I am unable to explain why Sukhwant is silent on Jacob's role in changing the plan, and Dacca might have been a paper option, it was not the objective up to the start of the war. Even the 'never-published official history' of the war says (p.280): "In the Eastern sector the strategy was to capture sufficient area bordering the Brahmaputra and Meghna river lines." This encompasses north-west and south-east East Bengal and is a good bit more than just the 20km depth all around East Pakistan that was the original and official target. But, it is also not Dacca.

Chapter 4

1. Sisson et al., pp.237–246, & Jyotsna Bakshi, 'Soviet Attitude towards Bangladesh Liberation Movement: A Study in Content Analysis of Soviet Press Author(s)', The Indian Journal of Political Science, Vol. 38, No. 2 (April–June 1977), pp.179–199.
2. Sisson et al., p.241.

Chapter 5

1. Hirandani, p.120, & *Weyers Flotten Taschenbuch 1977/78*, pp.363–364.
2. *Weyers Flotten Taschenbuch 1977/78*, pp.363–364.
3. For a detailed study of the PAF's opening strike, see Tufail, pp.20–29.
4. For a detailed study of the IAF operations over East Pakistan, see Jagan Mohan et al.
5. India actually had more aircraft than listed here, but trainers and temporarily non-operational aircraft are deducted.
6. Before the 1965 war with India, Pakistan was slated to receive Northrop F-5A/Bs as replacements for its worn out North American F-86 Sabres. This plan went out of the window due to the US arms embargo. Perhaps one of the biggest question marks about the PAF as of 1967–71 is why did Pakistan order MiG-19s (in their slightly improved Chinese variant Shenyang F-6) instead of more powerful MiG-21s (Shenyang F-7)? The answer is related to the fact that the Chinese experienced significant problems with launching domestic production of F-7s before breaking with the Soviets in 1960–61. Due to the Cultural Revolution, it was then only in the late 1960s that these were manufactured in any numbers and a few dozen were pressed into service with the People's Liberation Army Air Force (PLAAF).
7. The PAF took over six airfields constructed during the Second World War and kept them in working order. However, not expecting to get into another war with India, the Pakistanis failed to expand and fortify them properly. Moreover, it expected to crush the uprising in East Pakistan in just a couple of months. Ironically, the Pakistan Army did just that, and had India not stepped in, that would have been the end of the matter (at least temporarily). Once India launched its intervention, the PAF did not have enough aircraft to send them to the East – at least not without significantly weakening its air defences in the West.
8. Jagan Mohan et al., pp.378–379. Notably, not all these aircraft were committed to East Pakistan: 19 – all of them at Tezpur AB – were kept back in case of a Chinese intervention. Moreover, between 5 and 14 December 1971, the IAF withdrew Nos 7, 30 and 221 Squadrons from the Eastern to the Western Air Command. Eight Canberras based at Gorakhpur AB also possessed the endurance to fly combat sorties over West Pakistan, if required.
9. Jagan Mohan (author of multiple books about the history of the Indian Air Force), interview, March 2020.
10. Based on 'Enterprise Incident: Rhetoric, Reality and Pointers for the Contemporary Era', Journal of Defence Studies, Vol. 9, No. 2 (April–June 2015), pp.49–80; Krishnan, *No Way but Surrender*; J. McConnell & A. Kelly, *Superpower Naval Diplomacy in the Indo–Pakistan Crisis* (Arlington VA: Center for Naval Analysis, 1973); R. Mishra, 'Revisiting the 1971 "USS Enterprise Incident": Rhetoric, Reality and Pointers for the Contemporary Era', Journal of Defence Studies, Vol. 9 (2015), pp.49–80; P.W. Goldrick, *The U.S. Naval Demonstration in the Bay of Bengal during the 1971 India–Pakistan War* (self-published, 1979), pp.82–84; J. Goldrick, 'No Easy Answers: Development of the Navies of India, Pakistan, Bangladesh, and Sri Lanka, 1945–1996', Australian Maritime Affairs Vol. 2 (1997).
11. See McConnell et al.
12. R. Simha, '1971 War: How Russia sank Nixon's Gunboat Diplomacy', Russia Beyond (20 December 2011).
13. Similar is true for the content of an interview provided by Admiral Vladimir Kruglyakov (Commander of the 10th Battle Group/Pacific Fleet) to Russian TV, who wildly exaggerated: "The Commander-in-Chief's order was that our submarines should surface when the Americans appear. It was done to demonstrate to them that we had nuclear submarines in the Indian Ocean. So when our subs surfaced, they recognised us. In the way of the American Navy stood the Soviet cruisers, destroyers and nuclear submarines equipped with anti-ship missiles. We encircled them and trained our missiles at the Enterprise. We blocked them and did not allow them to close in on Karachi, Chittagong or Dacca." The Soviets could not have surrounded TF.74 in the Bay of Bengal because it was never there – especially not by the time their submarines arrived on the scene. The first Soviet submarine to reach the area, a nuclear-powered cruise-missile-armed boat of the Echo-class, showed up only after TF.74 had left for Sri Lankan waters.

14 US Navy, US Naval History and Heritage Command: Enterprise VIII (CVAN-65) 1971–1975 (8 July 2015).

Chapter 6
1   Agha H. Amin, e-mail conversation, 14 July 2020.
2   Sinh, *A Talent for War*.
3   Usual ORBATs cite a total of nine battalions within the 9th Infantry Division, Pakistan Army. However, one of these, the 21st Punjab, was dispersed in companies, while another was at Kushtia and therefore not available for the defence of Jhenda.
4   Mathew Varghese, 'Naval Operations During the 1971 War – A Retrospect', Salute.co.in (22 January 2015).
5   Prasad, pp.245–47.
6   A. Amin, 'Tank ambush at Kushtia', Defence Journal (November 2000).
7   This was a standard order by General Niazi applicable to all his troops in East Pakistan. It is difficult to see how any formation could withdraw after suffering 75 percent casualties, and the order ignored the reality of the state of the Pakistan Army, which was reviled, isolated, without air cover and facing great odds.
8   Prasad, pp.178–179.
9   To show how confused the Pakistan military leadership was, no one informed Brigadier Hayat, CO 57th Brigade, that the 314th Brigade had left for Dacca already on 7 December. It moved across the riverine terrain at night using boats, and hid during the day, thus saving itself from the keen attention of the IAF. Meanwhile, Pakistan Army helicopters flew dangerous missions (in the light of Indian air supremacy) to stock Khulna with ammunition and supplies for the defence. Clearly, HQ Dacca itself did not know that the ad-hoc brigade had decided to leave Khulna. A likely explanation for 314th Brigade abandoning Khulna was that the Bengal Area's three-battalion task force was advancing on the brigade's left flank.
10 Brigadier (ret.) Muhammad Hayat, 'Battle of Khulna, 10–17 December 1971', Defence Journal (March 1998). For comparison, one of the strangest accounts of the Battle of Khulna was written by M. Sadik, a journalist from Bangladesh ('Shiromoni Tank Battle', The Independent [Bangladesh], 16 December 2017). According to him, "The Shiromoni tank battle is one of the most glorious chapters in Bangladesh's Liberation War. In terms of magnitude and fierceness of fighting it can only be compared to the El Alamein tank battles in World War 2." Shiromoni is the industrial locality of Khulna, and the battle is described in colourful and heroic language. Supposedly, the Pakistanis had 32 tanks and the Indians had 10 or 11. The Pakistanis actually had only two dug-in M24s: when these destroyed an Indian tank, the Indians brought down heavy fire, destroying both of them – and that was the extent of the entire "tank battle". Another article (E. Haque, 'The bloody battle to free Khulna', TBS-News, 14 December 2019) says the battle is taught in 35 academies around the world, including India and Poland. It imagines a battle where the Rajputs are caught in an ambush as they advanced on Shiromoni, with 250–300 killed. The same article says that when the Indian commander refused to attack frontally, two majors of the Mukti Bahini rallied some of their men and charged the Pakistani defence line, vanishing into fire and smoke: when they re-emerged – after defeating the Pakistanis, of course – the Pakistani commander and his officers were all on their knees begging to surrender. Obviously, and unfortunately, exaggerations such as these destroy the credibility of the rebel resistance. They are more akin to superhero comic books than to history.
11 Unfortunately, and unfairly, after the war, the Hamadur–Rehman commission of inquiry indicted Brigadier Hayat for abandoning Jessore without a fight. It passes understanding how the inquiry remained unaware that Hayat was only following Niazi's instruction, that the 6th Punjab with two companies slowed down the Indian 9th Division to a crawl and how the 107th Brigade blocked the Indians from advancing further than the outskirts of Khulna. It stopped fighting only on Niazi's orders. There is speculation that Niazi wanted to save the 107th Brigade and its four battalions for the defence of Dacca. That said, at this point I would like to re-emphasise that neither the Indians nor the Pakistanis kept their records. The Pakistanis destroyed theirs before surrendering, the Indians some years later. A lot of what writers have said after the war is one-sided, and in attempting to make a coherent story, I have undoubtedly simplified some matters. Before blaming the GOC II Corps, Indian Army, it should be recalled that Manekshaw had no plan to take Dacca. To repeat, his idea was that India should take the port towns of Comilla and Khulna. Major General Jacob had correctly ridiculed this idea. It is plausible that GOC II Corps was doing only what Manekshaw wanted. No one could win argument against Jacob, so it might be that Manekshaw quietly told GOC II Corps to stick with his original plan. As such, none of the senior commanders of the corps can be blamed for their actions.
12 The recommended reference for this clash is Sidney Schanberg's reporting in *The Times*. He accompanied Indian troops to Jessore and Khulna, and his first-hand correspondent's accounts are reminiscent of Harry Brown's classic novel *A Walk in the Sun*.
13 The Reconnaissance and Support Battalion was usually broken up to provide extra firepower to the infantry. It could be deployed in platoons or companies.
14 Twenty-six years later, Major General Jacob, who in 1971 was Chief-of-Staff Eastern Command, severely criticised the II Corps for mishandling the battle following the fall of Jessore. Prone to speak his mind, he stressed the corps' job after Jessore was to cross the Madumati and then the Padma, heading for Dacca. Instead, it sent its 9th Division in a pointless diversion to Khulna. While the 4th Division did concentrate on the Padma River, it lost several days because of its overreaction when the 22nd Rajputs were ambushed at Kushtia. Writing in 2019, Lieutenant General Panag Singh, then a young captain, was bitter about the 9th Division's lost chance to be first into Dacca too (see Lieutenant General H. Panag, 'Why 1971 Battle of Khulna's Outcome made me respect Pakistan Army Brigadier Muhammad Hayat', The Print, 12 December 2019). Noting that the 9th Division suffered more casualties in the seven days of the Khulna battle than it had in the whole month prior, he concluded: "Dacca had never been assigned or discussed as an objective for II Corps that had 9 Infantry Division and 4 Infantry Division under its command. However, even to a young Captain like me, it was clear that having forced Pakistan's 9 Infantry Division to split and withdraw its two brigades (9 Infantry Division had only two brigades) towards the north and south, II Corps would now press on east to Dacca after leaving minimum forces to contain the two enemy brigades. Alas, II Corps remained enslaved to the 'force-on-force' strategy of attrition warfare and instead of racing to Dacca, it chased the Pakistani troops to the north and the south. This made it remain embroiled in high-intensity aimless tactical battles, which had no influence on the outcome of the war."

Chapter 7
1   The CO 16th Infantry Division, Major General Nazir Hussain Shah, later claimed even his divisional HQ was deployed as a part of the 205th's defences. This is highly unlikely as it would have not been conducive for his division's cohesion. Furthermore, the primary task of HQ troops is to lead and support their units: while they can and are equipped and trained to defend themselves, they are supposed to do so only if they cannot withdraw.
2   Major General Sukhwant Sigh, an acerbic and outspoken historian of the 1971 war, attributed this situation to the GOC Eastern Command, maintaining that no clear plan was made for XXXIII Corps. Actually, it seems that the relationship between him and Thapan was strained, and it remains unknown why Jacob – Eastern Army's aggressive and hard-driving Chief-of-Staff – had failed to straighten-out the situation.
3   Salik, p.152.
4   Ironically, Major General Sukhwant Singh subsequently stressed that the Indian planning for East Pakistan originally included no mobile warfare at all. This is contrary to recollections of younger officers, all of whom insisted that this was the only way to bypass Pakistani defence positions. Still, it does speak well of the Indian Army's leadership, for the flow of the campaign makes it clear that – contrary to its traditions based on the conservative British style of leadership – it was willing to listen to the advice of younger officers.
5   Gunapathy, 'Battle of Bogra'.

6   Prasad, p.547.
7   Ultimately, Major General Sukhwant Singh laconically noted that Hilli was "the only battle in the East where India tried to capture a fortified position by a frontal assault". Out of a sense of discretion, even though he wrote years after the event, his criticism is muted to the point that no lessons can be learned. The Indian Army was – and remains – a close-knit fraternity despite its size, which was then about 860,000 troops. The soldiers and officers are all long-service professionals, and loyalty prevents them from speaking their minds. Obviously, XXXIII Corps' strategy was severely faulty, but Major General Jacob avoided any criticism whatsoever. There are hints that GOC XXXIII Corps protested his orders from Eastern Command HQ, but GOC Eastern Command refused to listen. It has to be concluded that there was a lot of bad blood between the corps and army commanders; whether this existed earlier or developed after Eastern Command refused to take the corps' objections into account is not known.

Chapter 8

1   With hindsight, it is easy to condemn the GHQ of the Indian Army for not being bold enough. But, that is a post-fact fallacy. Such statements are only possible to make because we now know that China was not going to intervene. However, given that China and Pakistan were already very close allies, and that India planned nothing less than a disintegration of Pakistan – and thus a major change in the balance of power in South Asia – as of 1971, New Delhi had every reason to believe that Beijing would intervene. Thus, no matter how fond the Army chief actually was of Jacob, and that he had already conceded that – if possible – II Corps should make a run for Dacca, they remained insistent on the limited objectives.
2   To remain fair, one should consider the problem from the Army chief's perspective. He had already detached the 20th and 23rd Divisions from XXXIII and IV Corps, leaving Bhutan uncovered against a Chinese attack. The 6th Division had left a brigade in its area of responsibility, and was to lend its 9th Brigade to XXXIII Corps, but the division HQ and its 99th Brigade were to be ready to drop everything and deploy to Bhutan in case of need. The 5th and 2nd Divisions were the minimum protection for the North-East Frontier Agency. And the 2nd Division had already sent most of its divisional artillery to 8th Division, which – being a COIN-formation – had no artillery of its own. Army HQ was already running a serious risk; if it gave the 6th Division to the northern thrust and the Chinese attacked, Bhutan could be easily overrun, exposing the flanks of Sikkim and NEFA. The Army chief would then bear the responsibility for a major fiasco.
3   The term 'wing' was used to distinguish them from battalions: they had only three instead of four companies. The Pakistan Rangers usually guarded West Pakistan's plains frontier with India, together with the Border Security Force (which had six companies to a battalion). Like India's Assam Rifles, used for the north-east India frontier and internal security, the Rangers were staffed by regular officers.
4   Sukhwant Singh points out that even during their retreat, whenever the Pakistanis halted to fight, they managed to impose a further 24-hour delay.
5   When he found none had arrived, he grabbed file photographs of a big air drop and gave them to the media as the real thing. For showing initiative, he got a dressing down by his superiors. Fortunately for the officer, the head of India's Research and Analysis Wing was in the room. While the Air Force officers were frowning, the PRO saw that the RAW Chief was smiling and approvingly nodding his head. A very short time thereafter, the PRO found he had a new job, working for RAW. These media pictures also worked to convince Lieutenant General Niazi that a whole para brigade had arrived outside Dacca, and this – by his own admission – deepened his despondency and sapped his will to resist.
6   Jagan Mohan et al., *Eagles over Bangladesh*, pp.378–91.
7   P. Rao, 'With a Damaged Tail Plane over DZ at Tangail', bharat-rakshak.com (18 November 2018).

Chapter 9

1   Salik, p.160.
2   Unless stated otherwise, based on Salik, *Witness to Surrender*.
3   At the time of surrender, on 16 December 1971, all three major elements of the PA 14th Division were concentrated in the Sylhet area. Somehow, they managed to hold out until the ceasefire, although exhausted by 25 days of heavy fighting. However, it is almost certain that the Indians were also worn out. Moreover, they knew they had cut the 14th Division into two, and thus neutralised it as an offensive force. Most likely, seeing little point in taking further casualties by overrunning Sylhet, they left the Pakistanis to their own devices. Ultimately, some 6,500 Pakistani officers and other ranks in Sylhet were to surrender on 17 December, one day after the ceasefire.
4   Based on Jagan Mohan and Chopra, pp.380–381, 387.
5   The Rajput and Rajputana Rifles were two separate infantry regiments, while the 31st Jat and 32nd Mahar were in COIN configuration (i.e., light infantry).
6   Gill, pp.31–32.
7   Dapon Ratuk Ngawang, 'The Tibetans who fought the 1971 War', Rediff.com (10 January 2012).

Chapter 10

1   Farman Ali, pp.162–176.
2   It is also evident from other documents that Bhutto worked against his own government at the UN when a ceasefire was being proposed because he wanted the generals humiliated and discredited, opening the way for his accession to the presidency. In retrospect, it is also evident that the prisoners of war could have come back by mid-1972 but for Bhutto, by then President, importuning Gandhi not to release them. His excuse was that he wanted to build a democratic Pakistan and the return of the troops would strengthen the military. This is a clear illustration of the actual tragedy of Pakistan – valid for 1971, as for our days too: its leaders constantly put their petty ambitions before the country.
3   Rao Farman Ali Khan, p.202.

Chapter 11

1   Aurora, 'The Fall of Dacca'; Shahnawaz Khan, '54 Indian PoWs of 1971 War still in Pakistan', Daily Times, Lahore (11 October 2011); Salunke, Pakistani Prisoners of War, p.10.
2   The question of power and might was not the only issue: religion played an important role too. All the powerful mullahs of Pakistan have considered democracy to be 'non-Islamic'. Indeed, when President Yahya visited East Pakistan to negotiate a transfer of power to Mujib in February 1971, upon seeing the pro-independence fervour of the population, he observed to one of his closest advisors: "If Jinnah was willing to accept two independent Muslim states, who am I to decline?"
3   Zaki, *Through the Lens of Operational Art*.
4   *Hamoodur Rahman Commission*, pp.50–54.

ABOUT THE AUTHOR

Ravi Rikhye studied international military affairs for 10-years before writing his first paper. Over the last 60 years he has authored and co-authored over 30 books, many of these for the Government of India (though a number are unpublished). He is currently completing his seventh master's degree (in Intelligence Management), and hoping to undertake his first doctorate. This is his first installment for Helion's *Asia@War* series.